JOSÉ LIMÓN

JOSÉ LIMÓN

Edited by June Dunbar

Routledge
Taylor & Francis Group

NEW YORK AND LONDON

First published in paperback in 2002 by
Routledge
29 West 35th Street
New York, NY 10001
www.routledge-ny.com

Published in Great Britain by
Routledge
11 New Fetter Lane
London EC4P 4EE
www.routledge.co.uk

Routledge is an imprint of the Taylor & Francis Group
Printed in the United States of America on acid-free paper.

10 9 8 7 6 5 4 3 2 1

Cataloging-in-Publication Data is available from the Library of Congress.

ISBN 0-415-96581-0 (pbk.)

CONTENTS

List of Plates   vii

Introduction   ix

1. Artistic Succession and Leadership in
   a Modern Dance Company   1
   Carla Maxwell

2. Dancers Are Musicians Are Dancers   9
   José Limón

3. The Dance Heroes of José Limón   19
   Norton Owen

4. Paulina Regina   27
   Charles D. Tomlinson

5. Voices of the Body   37
   Betty Jones

6. My Dance Family   45
   Charles H. Woodford

7. Thomas Skelton, Lighting Designer   53
   Jennifer Tipton

8. Lucas Hoving and José Limón: Radical Dancers   59
   Ann Murphy

9. Limón in Mexico; Mexico in Limón   71
   Ann Vachon

10. *Mazurkas:* Origins, Choreography, Significance   85
    Michael Hollander

11. The 1954 Limón Company Tour to South America:
Goodwill Tour or Cold War Cultural Propaganda?   97
Melinda Copel

12. The Essence of Humanity: José Limón After a Half Century   113
Sarah Stackhouse

13. Remembering José Limón   127
June Dunbar

Appendix I: José Limón Chronology   133
Compiled by Norton Owen

Appendix II: Chronological List of Works Choreographed
by José Limón   137
Compiled by Lynn Garafola

Appendix III: Alphabetical List of Works Choreographed
by José Limón   153

Notes on Contributors   157

Index   163

LIST OF PLATES

Carla Maxwell.   1
Simon Sadoff, conductor, pianist and musical director
   of the Limón Company, taking a bow with José Limón.   17
Harald Kreutzberg.   19
Charles Weidman, Doris Humphrey and José Limón
   at Mills College, 1933.   22
Pauline Lawrence Limón and José Limón seated in the studio
   of their house in New Jersey.   32
Betty Jones with student at Théâtre Contemporain de la
   Danse, Paris.   42
Charles Weidman, Doris Humphrey, José Limón and Pauline
   Chellis with Charles Humphrey Woodford at Blairstown,
   New Jersey.   46
Thomas Skelton.   55
Lucas Hoving and José Limón in *The Emperor Jones*.   63
Lucas Hoving and José Limón in rehearsal of *The Traitor*.   67
José Limón and dancers from the Academia de la Danza
   Mexicana in *Tonantzintla*.   80
Michael Hollander, Betty Jones, Lola Huth, Lucy Venable,
   Harlan McCallum, Ruth Currier and Chester Wolenski
   in *Mazurkas*.   90
Louis Falco and Sarah Stackhouse in *A Choreographic Offering*.   115
José Limón, left, sitting on stone wall in front of his house
   at "the farm" in Stockton, New Jersey.   131

INTRODUCTION

The chapters in this book have, for the most part, been written by people who have not previously published articles or books about José Limón. My wish was to invite people who knew him well or had worked with him in one capacity or another or who could write with insight about a specific aspect of his company or his life. I also wanted to include texts that discussed his artistic collaborators, Pauline Lawrence and Tom Skelton. Both were crucial in bringing his vision of theater to reality by designing costumes and light for his dances. Since Simon Sadoff, José's valued music director of many years, is no longer living, I decided to let José speak for himself about his ideas about music.

June Dunbar

1

ARTISTIC SUCCESSION AND LEADERSHIP IN A MODERN DANCE COMPANY

Carla Maxwell

Carla Maxwell. Photo copyright by Beatriz Schiller.
José Limón Dance Foundation Archives.

This year, 1997, The Limón Company is celebrating its 50th anniversary. For 25 of those 50 years it has been without its founding director and main creative force, José Limón. Next year our history will begin to record more years without José than there were with him. It is astounding to me to look back and realize these facts. Even as we live through this momentous year we are being propelled into the next millennium and our history seems to take on even greater significance. In this very special year, it is time to look back and reflect on how we managed this past quarter of a century, and where we find ourselves on the threshold of our next half century.

Limón's personal career as a creative and performing artist, for the most part, follows the prototypes of the early founders of modern dance in this country. But the last 25 years without him don't fit neatly into any pre-determined formula. They are our own unique history, and tell the story of the emergence of what has become a paradigm in the dance field in terms of artistic succession. Let me give you some background, and describe the circumstances surrounding José's death.

On December 2, 1972, José Limón passed away after a three year battle with cancer. His wife and artistic help-mate for over thirty years, Pauline Lawrence Limón, also suffering from cancer, died the year before him. José left us as he lived, fighting for the dance and creating. His last two works, *Orfeo* and *Carlota*, premiered just two months before his death.

José left an active company of sixteen dancers, who had a full year's work already scheduled. This included a month-long tour of the Soviet Union, a month's engagement in Paris, extensive domestic touring and a six-week summer residency. José did not, however, leave anyone to be in charge artistically of this company, nor was any clear provision made in his will for the care or continuance of his dances. He did not have a school of his own, having taught for most of his career in established institutions such as The Juilliard School and the American Dance Festival. At the time of his death, the company did not have a studio of its own. Rehearsal space was rented, or was lent by the institutions where he taught.

When José died, there was no strong organizational structure in place to support the company. His attitude concerning the business part of his art contributed in part to this state of affairs. He had what we would consider today a rather naive way of thinking about money and funding; believing that if he was good enough someone would come forward and give him the necessary funds or lead him to resources. And, indeed, he was honored in his lifetime with awards, grants, extensive tours, and recognition for his creativity, performance abilities and work for the field. But this did not encourage José to pursue benefactors or people with funding strategies. So, at the time of his death there was no structure for succession in place, nor anyone to come forward to offer the necessary financial assistance to carry on.

Until a few years before her death, José's wife, Pauline Lawrence Limón took care of every aspect of running his company, including designing his costumes and attending to many aspects of the productions. This left José free to concentrate his energies on creating, teaching and performing. But José and Pauline did not feel compelled to keep up with the administrative structures being developed in the rest of the field. So even though it was 1972 when José died, and he had incorporated in order to receive grants and donations, there was no active Board of Directors and no administrative staff except for a booking agent. Neither was there any other structure in place to substitute for this personal way of operating a company.

Understandably, many of the people who were close to José and who might have helped with the continuance of his work, were so distraught by his death that they found it very difficult to be involved with the company at that time. It was only after many years that some of these people were able to give their emotional and artistic support.

The climate in the dance community was such that no one believed that a company, and in particular a modern dance company, could continue after the death of its founder. It was thought that we might finish out the work scheduled and then disband. There were also disputes in the language in José's will, so what may have seemed obvious in terms of taking care of his artistic legacy, turned into a legal entanglement that remained unresolved for fourteen years. It was not until 1986 that all rights to Limón's work were finally held indisputably with The Limón Foundation.

This was the environment in which we found ourselves in 1972. No ground work had been laid for this major transition in the life of The Limón Company; not by the dance community, not within the structure and organization of Limón's foundation, and not by José himself. There were no prototypes to emulate and no belief that we could succeed if we decided to try.

During that first year of work after José's death, everyone involved with the company realized that we were there for more than José as a person or artist, and that if we disbanded, another lifetime of work by a creative genius would disappear. There had to be a living entity to carry his vision into the future. We also realized that our company embraced much more than just the work of Limón. It also included the work of his teachers and mentors, Doris Humphrey and Charles Weidman, and those that inspired them. What was left to us was much more than a repertory of dances. There was a technique, an aesthetic, a philosophy about dance and theater; in fact, an entire tradition!

Charles Tomlinson, José's friend and a costume designer who had worked with the company, was the first to have the belief and the foresight that we must go on. It was he who planted the seed in our spirits that it might be possible. Already in the last months that José was alive he found new comprehensive management. When José died he instigated a search for a new artistic director. Daniel Lewis, then a leading soloist with the company and an assistant to José was asked to be Acting Artistic Director during the search. For those first eight months Danny and Chuck worked endlessly to bring some order to the chaos in which we found ourselves.

In July of 1973, Ruth Currier was asked to fill the role of Artistic Director. During her five-year tenure, she established the foundation's first active Board of Directors, started to untangle the myriad legal problems surrounding the rights to José's works, and set the groundwork of our artistic platform. She helped us to define, in body and words, our mission as an organization, and to separate vision, aesthetics, points of view and choreography from the personalities who fostered them. In her quiet way she opened the door, and made possible the beginnings of our rebirth.

During these years, other questions were raised. Were the works of Limón worth saving, or were they just vehicles for the charismatic performances of Limón and his contemporaries? Could these dances be brought to life by anyone other than Limón and his peers? (Interestingly, this last question was also being asked of Martha Graham as she passed on her own roles, while she was still alive and active.) It is my guess that, in José's lifetime his great choreographic talent was eclipsed by the fact that he was such a compelling and phenomenal performer. It has taken these many years to balance the memory of his powerful presence with the realization that he was also one of our great choreographers.

At the same time that people were praising Limón's accomplishments and saying that no one could ever replace him, they were questioning his viability as an enduring creative artist. In 1977, when Ruth resigned and I was asked to assume artistic responsibility for the company, I was confronted with such remarks as: "Why should the Limón Company exist now that *The Moor's Pavane* is in the repertory of some of our major ballet companies?" Or, "Yes, it is the mission of the National Endowment for the Arts to safeguard our national heritage, but right now we don't have any category that your company could fit into. Perhaps when Mr. Balanchine or Miss Graham die we'll have to address the issue of artistic succession and a company's ability to continue without its founder." (Ironically, as late as 1991, when Graham did pass away, we saw the publication of a major article in *The New York Times*, which not only questioned how a company could go on without its founding director, but asked, should it?) But most often I would be asked, "What makes you think that The Limón Company can survive? Who, in your situation has ever succeeded before? Why are you even trying?"

It was clear that there would be little help from the dance community. It was up to us to prove that our tradition was worth saving, and show how it could be done. We had to create our own rules. All of this forced us into intense self-examination. What do we represent in the panoply of American dance? What is the essence of what we want to pass on? How might we evolve this aesthetic and bring it into the future? All of the answers came through process, and trial and error problem-solving.

In 1946 when Limón had formed his own company, he had asked Doris Humphrey to be the Artistic Director of the group and share in the training of the dancers and the creation of new work. This was already precedent-breaking for that time, because forming a modern dance company was considered a solo endeavor. One was responsible for everything: all the choreography, the training of the dancers and performing as well. So from the beginning, Limón created the concept of a repertory company, and over the years he presented not only his and Doris' work, but that of some of his company members as well, including Lucas Hoving, Ruth Currier, Pauline Koner and Louis Falco.

In 1965 José's broadness and generosity of vision was recognized when he was asked to be the Artistic Director for the short-lived American Dance Theater - the first major attempt at an American modern dance repertory company to house the classics of modern dance and commission new works. But the dance field was not ready for such a phenomenon and the project folded after two seasons. This idea, however, was ever present in our heritage and became the basis of our future endeavors after José's death. Today, we have redefined this concept of a modern dance repertory company to be one rooted in a strong tradition, presenting classics from that tradition, and commissioning new works that are compatible with that aesthetic.

As we explored the issues of what we were and how we would continue, we were again challenged in our progress. We seemed to be carrying "the baggage of the survivor"; we were always referred to as the first company that survived the death of its founder, and, therefore, how we had evolved was not addressed. We thought that this attitude had started to change after 15 years, but even as late as 1991, the title of a feature article on the company in *Dance Magazine* was "Life After Death". And of course, there has never been any consensus from our critics concerning what our mission is and how we're pursuing it. While one critic saw our efforts as "a new, even tenuous, direction that bears little relationship to modern dance's own perception of itself in the past", [that we had] "blurred our own profile", [and had warned that this might lead us to a] "loss of identity",[1] others praised our "artistic integrity"[2] [and saw us] "'flourishing" in our founder's absence. [3] We have long since stopped trying to please our critics. The artistic choices of each company are its own to make. We were walking the fine line between maintaining the integrity of our roots, and simultaneously allowing for growth and change. The latitude to do this was something initially denied us by the dance community. The personal image of José was always stamped in their minds and it was nearly impossible for critics to allow us breathing room to be who we were.

There is a great irony in our story. José actually addressed the issue of artistic continuance in relationship to Doris Humphrey, and yet he did so little to ensure the continuation of his own work. In 1946 when he was forming his company and inviting her to be his artistic director, he was offering that his company to be the repository for her work and the means for it to continue after her own group folded. Moreover, José spent his entire life fighting for American dance: fighting for both his tradition and the creative spirit. He was compelled to do it, and at the same time he felt privileged to be recognized as an artist. In an article in *Dance Observer*, January 1947, entitled "Young Dancers Speak Their Views", José said the following: "The opinion is sometimes expressed that American dance will disappear along with its contemporary personalities when they retire from the stage. I do not believe this. The American dance has already known approximately three generations of artist exponents. Each generation has contributed to its impetus, its power, and its expressiveness. This sort of dance is inevitable. It is actually compelled out of us by our great continent with its crude magnificences. It is not merely a style or idiom. It is a potent idea. And when its contemporary personalities retire the idea will persist."

This strong belief in the power of dance as a life force is also part of our tradition and an element which has contributed strongly to our continuance. José and his contemporaries were the vessels through which we now can see the birth of an art form and an aesthetic, pure dance: passionate, theatrical, inspired by life's challenges, utterly human, and shaped by form, physicality and musicality. José once wrote that the art he wanted to create would combine the utmost passion with the strictest discipline. For Limón, dance and dance making was a ritual and a means of communication, and therefore the form is paramount. All elements must be part of the whole. These goals are also part of the tradition that we carry and greatly influence me in choosing choreographers to be included in our repertory.

The idea of artistic succession implies to me an act of going forward, an act of evolution and creativity. It is not a fixed place that keeps repeating itself. It is a bringing of our past into the present, and allowing it to change its shape as it moves forward. José very much supported and believed in this idea. For one thing he did not want his technique codified; he wanted it to grow and develop. There is no rigid, set Limón class and no two teachers will impart the movement principles in the same way. José was always encouraging people to find the dance that was in them; to find their own way and trust the creative process. At the same time he fought vigorously for the tradition handed down to him by Doris Humphrey. He felt that the past should be "revered", not "embalmed". In speaking of tradition, he said, "There is a great difference between a pantheon and a mausoleum."[4]

In dance, the act of creation is more dependent on personalities than in any other art form. A choreographer might conceptualize his work alone, but to actually create, he needs other people. Perhaps this is why we are so reluctant to let go of the creative life forces who are our choreographers, and find it so difficult to separate them from their work.

When someone dies, first we mourn the loss of that person's physical presence, and then we start to look at the essence of what that person represented for us. We each have our own process of deciphering what can stay with us, and what is lost forever. And so, in looking at our dance heritage, we must do the same. We must recognize the essence of a creation, as well as the physical structure in which it was created. We must separate the performance from the choreography, the work from the personality. In looking at the dance and deciding what it is we want to save, we must also keep reaffirming what it is that makes dance the art form that it is.

I am always struck by the mystery and the energy of the remarkable field of which we are a part. Dance is one of the oldest means of communication. It is primitive, unconscious, intangible; not intellectual or verbal. It can only be passed on from body energy to body energy, from soul to soul. It, therefore, is ever-changing and ever-evolving, while remaining human, vital, and honest. Movement doesn't lie. You can't hold it in you hand or hang it on the wall. It is a life experience and exists only for the moment in which it happens. Each performance must be painstakingly rediscovered. The dance makes no guarantees and is the most fickle of lovers. Even with all of our present technology there is no way to fully capture the thrill and illusiveness of a live dance performance. At best we create a new medium for expression, that of dance for film or video.

Ours is a youth-oriented, "NOW" culture, a disposable, throw-away society. We don't take time to integrate the past into our lives. I, for one, find that very frightening. If we as a dance community value the contributions made by our artists, then we must find the measures to ensure their legacies. Especially now, in a political climate which views the arts as superfluous, we must find the means to strengthen and extend what those outside our dance community perceive as the power and function of dance.

It is now over 25 years since José died and we have proved that it is possible for a company to continue successfully after the death of its founder. We have not always made the choices expected of us, and this has made our critics uncomfortable. But we have been "continuing", "evolving", "succeeding", those good words that the dictionary uses to describe "succession." The Company has received international recognition as a modern dance repertory company and there is renewed interest in Limón's work. As well, we have developed a project to create new dances and save masterpieces of American dance, in addition to works by Limón, Humphrey and Weidman. We have done so by recognizing and defining the legacy left to us, and by working together, many generations of Limón artists, administrators and educators, to perpetuate what was a gift to us all. We have been inspired by the "potent idea" that is our tradition, and no contribution has been too small to ensure that future generations will also understand and be inspired by this heritage. What could be a greater testament to this combined effort than this wonderful collection of essays about Limón and his work in this book.

As so many of the seminal figures in our dance history pass away, it is time for us all to reflect and consider our history; what it has brought us thus far, and how it can help us move forward into the next millennium.

Notes

1. Anna Kisselgoff, *The New York Times*, January 7, 1979.
2. Suzanne Walther, *New Haven Register*, February 24, 1980.
   Myron Galloway, Montreal, *The Express*, October 1980.
3. Carole Beers, *The Seattle Times*, December 14, 1980.
4. The Juilliard Review, Convocation Address by José Limón, October 5, 1966.

2

DANCERS ARE MUSICIANS ARE DANCERS

CONVOCATION ADDRESS GIVEN ON OCTOBER 5, 1966 AT JUILLIARD SCHOOL OF MUSIC

José Limón

It is my honor and pleasure on this occasion to address you. President Mennin asked that I talk about my experience as a worker in the arts, and it has occurred to me that it might be of interest to you if I chose as my subject music and dance, musicians and dancers, composers and choreographers. This I have done for reasons very obvious to all of us here present, but mainly for another motive. I have always maintained that musicians are dancers, and that dancers can be good dancers only when they are also good musicians. This does not mean that a composer need perform, literally and physically, all the arduous vocabulary of the dancer, nor that the dancer need be proficient with a violin, kettledrum or harp. No.

I have always known certain music to dance, literally, as well as figuratively. The dance has been called the matrix of the arts. Early in our adventure as humans on this planet, very early, even before language was invented, as pre-humans, or sub-humans, or humanoids, we had that supremely instinctual urge and capacity to dance. From this was born percussion and song and music and ritual and painting and sculpture, and from these, architecture and poetry. But all this is another story. Let me, today, only point to that supremely choreographic composer, that incomparable dancer of the spirit, J. S. Bach. He dances not only in his French suites, and English suites, and partitas and sonatas for the various instruments, with their chaconnes, minuets, courantes, sarabandes, allemandes, gigues, and other dance forms, but he could not and did not exclude the dance from the cantatas and oratorios. Dance, as you know, is of all kinds and categories. There is a dance for every single human experience. What, may I ask, can we call the impassioned procreative act; what else but dance is the convulsion of birth; what is the perpetual delight of infancy and childhood but a dance; and what of the frenetic rituals of adolescence; and the sober solemnities of maturity, the weddings, academic processions, inaugurations, coronations, funerals; what are these but the dances with which we are conceived, are born, grow,

live and die? All this is dance, both profane and sacred. Bach contains it
in all his music, whether secular or religious. He was irrepressively a
dancer. Embedded in the cantatas, the oratorios, among the chorales,
the arias, and the recitatives, placed there with the most consummate
mastery of drama and theater that compels you with the irresistible
kinesthetic impetus which is dance.

If you don't believe me, I recommend that you hear the cantata, *Ich
Habe Genug*. This sublime work contains some of the most profoundly
moving of Bach's music. It probes deeply into the human spirit. The
opening aria, the following recitative, the second aria and recitative
express the renunciation of the burdens and sins of this life and a yearn-
ing for union with God. It is solemn and devastatingly beautiful music.
The concluding aria sees a vision of death as a deliverer, with joy and
peace as an eternal reward. How does Bach, the master dramatist and
imagist, give you this concluding ecstatic vision? Being a great dancer
and a great choreographer, he gives you an intoxicating dance. In 3/4
tempo. A lovely waltz. This, remember, in the year 1732 *anno domini*.
Almost one hundred years before the waltz came into being. He sets the
basso, oboe, string orchestra, continuo and your being to dancing. This
cantata was composed for the Feast of the Purification, and J. S. Bach
could think of no better way to conclude, to resolve, to purify, than
through the dance. Or perhaps we can say that, being a great musician
and composer, he could not refrain from the dance.

Dancers, fully aware that the art of music has far outdistanced the
dance in dimension, repute and achievement, have attempted to "free"
the dance from its subservience to music. It is true that the dance has had
its ups and downs, and there is evidence that when the dance was at a
low ebb, it made use of inferior music. Whether a degraded dance engen-
dered bad music or whether inconsequential music was the cause of a
decadence in the dance, I do not know. The truth is that they have co-
exisred as accomplices, to the dismay and horror of dancers concerned
with the status of their art. The dream of these artists, in their search for
a "liberation," was a dance without music. The dance was to be made
self-sufficient. It would create its own music and its own rhythms. It is
said that the great Nijinsky was a precursor in this as in other aspects of
the impetus towards the dance as a modern art of the twentieth century.
As his mind and his reason tottered on the brink of a tragic insanity, during moments of lucidity, he would dance his vision of a dance never
before seen, an utterance from the depths of his tormented spirit, performed in a hypnotic silence. These rituals, witnessed by a handful of
invited spectators are said to have had a majestic and terrible beauty.

Doris Humphrey and Martha Graham, in the early days of the
American dance, when they were pregnant with an indigenous art,

conceived it as gloriously free of the dead hand of an effete and decayed past. Doris Humphrey created dances, almost symphonic in dimension, entirely without musical accompaniment. In rejecting the metronomic tempi of the musicians, she searched for the rhythms and phrases inherent in the human entity with its breathing, its muscular dynamics and emotive range. This was a manner of looking at dance quite distinct from that which accepts conformity to the 3/4, 2/4, 4/4, 6/8 time designations of the musicians. She accomplished some revolutionary works, the repercussions of which are with us to this day. I was privileged, as a young member of her company, to perform in some of these. I was able to observe how her audacity opened new horizons to the human gesture. I was astonished when, one day, she returned to J. S. Bach. To the *Passacaglia and Fugue in C Minor*. Bach, her first love. And to contemporary composers. To Wallingford Riegger, with whom she collaborated on a titanic trilogy, the apogee of her career, *New Dance*, *Theater Piece* and *With My Red Fires*. One day she said to me, "I have learned much in the search for a dance that can stand by itself. I know that the dance can never produce works to equal the symphonies, sonatas and oratorios of the musicians until it can learn to do so. I have succeeded in part; I have failed in part. I have learned that dance and music belong together. But they must meet as equals, not one subservient to the other. They must complement each other."

This she proceeded to prove in a long succession of works of dazzling choreographic mastery and dramatic power. She was another great musician-dancer.

Relations between the musician and the dancer have always been interesting. There has never been a dull moment. The confrontation between these two has not always been face to face. Often a living dancer performs to a score by a defunct composer.

Isadora Duncan, this audacious phenomenon who electrified and scandalized the first decades of this century, would dance, solo, to entire symphonies of Tchaikovsky and Schubert. She was the center of much controversy. There were those who reviled her as a shameless amateur and dilettante. To others, she was a miracle incarnate. In any case, her method of dealing with music was to "interpret" it. There was apparently a good deal of the improvisatory. A musical work was never "interpreted" the same way twice. She had the power to sustain, single handed, so to speak, a performance which left her audiences in a state verging on a pandemonium of adoration. One interesting detail is recounted: to one of the adagio movements, I forget whether in the *Fifth* or the *Pathetique* of Tchaikovsky, she would begin extreme upstage center, walk slowly forward, so slowly that it was not clear how she was moving, raising her shapely arms. This simple gesture took the entire movement of the symphony to perform. At the end of the movement, she had reached the footlights. The effect was hypnotic. The luminous vision of the half-naked dancer, half bacchante, half goddess, was overwhelming. Except to her detractors, who complained that this wasn't dancing.

I asked Doris Humphrey, who would always speak of Pavlova and Nijinsky with reverence and adoration, if it was really true that these two lived up to the legend that has grown about them. She said that it was true and much more. In these two, she saw perfection. Flawless artistry. Then came the supreme accolade, "They did not dance to music. They were music," she said.

We have seen for decades, and we see now Martha Graham, one of the towering artists of the dance, use the music of her contemporaries to create fabulous theater. Her fecund creativity has taken movement and gesture, music, decor, lighting and costuming to a magical synthesis. The visual is always so completely arresting that it is only on subsequent seeings that one becomes aware of the music, and the superb use that is made of it. She has given us an apotheosis of art in America.

And here is a curious thing about the relationship between dancer and musician. It has been said often that on first viewing a dance, if you are fully aware of the musical accompaniment, the dance has failed to interest and absorb you as it should. It bored you. It was too long, too tedious, too repetitious, badly composed, badly danced. You took refuge in attending to the music. All dancers and choreographers have had this bitter truth to contend with. Music for dance is successful and effective only when it has been so skillfully utilized that you are not aware of it as a separate component or ingredient. It has blended so perfectly that you are not aware where the dance ceases to be and the music begins.

You realize, of course, that not all music can be danced to. That is obvious. Not that dancers haven't tried, at various times, to tread where angels have feared to. As caustic critics of the predilections and weaknesses of dancers and choreographers have pointed out, nothing is sacred. There was much vituperation when Doris Humphrey had the temerity to compose a dance to the majestic *Passacaglia and Fugue* of Bach. Of this case, as it happens, the dance did not do an injustice to the music, but on its own terms was equally majestic. Isadora Duncan, in her memoirs, repeatedly made allusion to her dream of making a dance to the *Ninth Symphony* of Beethoven. This desire seemed to haunt and obsess her. She died with this goal unattained. It would have been a most interesting thing for the world to have seen the result of her attempt.

Leonide Massine made choreographic settings to the Tchaikovsky *Fifth*, the Brahms *Fourth*, the Beethoven *Seventh* and the *Fantastique* of Berlioz for the Ballets Russes de Monte Carlo. Despite the inevitably arresting and exciting results, grave doubts were voiced that he should have done so. Unlike the music of Bach, these works in the romantic idiom seem to leave no room, or at least not much room, for the dancer.

Possibly the most felicitous choices, in recent years of extant music, have been made by our distinguished colleague here at Juilliard, Antony Tudor, in selecting and using superbly Schoenberg's *Verklärte Nacht* for his masterpiece *Pillar of Fire* and Chausson's *Poème* for Violin and Orchestra for his exquisite *Lilac Garden*.

One of the delights of the contemporary ballet repertory is the wit and wistful whimsicality of Agnes de Mille. Her use of the native folk dance and its music is always a refreshing contrast to the cool classicism or impassioned romanticism of her colleagues. Her works have a simplicity and ingenuousness which derive from her sources. In *Rodeo*, with the help of a fine score by Aaron Copland, she brought to brilliant synthesis the elements of the American folk dance. Miss de Mille is a wit of the first order. When asked by an interviewer, among many other things, what was her approach to music, she answered, "My approach to music is with scissors and paste."

My wife as a young girl just out of high school, as a talented pianist, found herself playing the piano for dancers' rehearsals. She speaks of these days as completely fascinating. A new and exciting world, the world of art and glamour was opened to her. One rehearsal she finds memorable. She was playing for a famous dancer. The concluding bars of a solo passage were causing grave trouble. The dance and the music just simply would not end simultaneously. This happened over and over again. In utter exasperation the dancer stalked to the piano, pointed a trembling finger at the music, and demanded to know why the final chord was not being played. My wife explained that there was no such chord, that she was playing the music as it was on the paper. The dancer, by now very irritated, pointed to a mark on the music and demanded, "What's that?" "That's a rest," said my wife. "Well, play it anyway!" My wife did. She played the rest.

Wallingford Riegger came to Doris Humphrey's studio to make notes on the music he was to write for her *New Dance*. Their collaboration resulted in the first of a monumental trilogy which I have already mentioned. The dance, incidentally, was already composed. Doris was determined that this "new" dance would originate and develop from the dancer's instrument, its dynamics, its range and rhythms. She and the dancers would demonstrate phrases, accents, stresses, suspensions, ritards. Mr. Riegger sat with his back to the studio mirrors, making notations on his music paper. Doris' little boy, Humphrey, aged three years, was an interested spectator. He was a well behaved child and seemed to enjoy watching rehearsals occasionally. Mr. Riegger became aware that the child was looking over his shoulder at the curious hieroglyphics being put down on the music paper. My wife, who was also present, noticed that the composer's pencil continued its activity over the page, but imperceptively the notes work on a strange and unmusical aspect. One line, one curve followed another, and before the absorbed and fascinated eyes of the little boy, a mouse, complete with ears and whiskers and tail squatted on its hind legs. There is no limit to the lengths to which a composer will go to astound, astonish, impress and enchant!

Musicians who play or conduct for dancers do so at their own peril. There is that perennial and seemingly irreconcilable controversy over what constitutes the right tempo. As you can imagine, what is right for one person is not for another. What is right in the morning can become just the opposite by late afternoon or evening. A tempo agreed upon at a studio rehearsal can go completely to hell because of nerves on an opening night. Then there is the cleavage in the comprehension of tempo by a human being who understands it from, say a piano bench, or from the conductor's podium and one who feels it in the more extended, more spatial way of the dancer. One of the most inspired audacities of the human species is the temerity to take eternity, which is forever, yesterday, and forever, tomorrow, and the ever elusive instant which is the present, and force it into a beat, a rhythm, a phrase. All manners of ingenuities have gone into chronometric devices. We agree about seconds, minutes, hours, days, weeks, months, years, centuries, millenia and eons. But there is still that baffling and subtle human unpredictability which sets us apart from machines. I have known conferences between dancers and conductors where the arbiter was a metronome and/or a stop watch. Agreements have been made. Notations on scores carefully written: such and such a number equals such and such a note. Come the performance and all this is as if nothing had been arbitrated, agreed, notated, and rehearsed to the point of mutual exhaustion. A very sweaty confrontation behind the scenes is as follows:

"What in God's name happened to the tempo"? demands the frustrated dancer. "What was wrong? I thought I gave it to you precisely as you wanted it," replies the conductor.

"Well, it was twice too fast." (or too slow as the case may be).

Musicians sometimes claim that the dancer hasn't the slightest idea of what it is he wants. On a certain performance, if he's feeling fine and he can sustain jumps much higher, he naturally wants a slower tempo. If he's low in energy, on the other hand, he wants the tempo just a tiny bit faster. But how is the poor musician to know all this? Can he read minds? Well, no, but dancers say he can do much better, he can read bodies, and their movements. Which means that he must feel and identify with the sheer mechanics and athleticism of the dancer's craft. He must get to know, just as though he himself were doing it, the pulse, the duration, of a given movement. On the other hand, a good dancer must have the capacity to give with minor and inconsequential deviation from an accustomed or desired beat.

Apropos of this, I have had the honor of performing with distinguished composers at the baton. Heitor Villa-Lobos was commissioned by the Empire State Festival to compose the score for *The Emperor Jones*. I was to do the choreography and dance the title role. The Maestro and I began work in February. The work was to be premiered in July. We had frequent conferences in the living room of his hotel suite. We discussed an adaptation of the O'Neill drama. I would rehearse for him passages in the dance, Jones' arrogance, bravado, terror, dissolution, etc., and Senor Villa-Lobos would go to the piano and play a phrase. We would put it together and arrive at a consensus. He spoke Portuguese and I answered in Spanish and we understood each other perfectly, most of the time. But when both the Iberian languages failed us, he would make himself understood by jumping up and dancing what he meant, or I would go to the piano and bang out a rhythm or a discord. You see here the two arts working as they should and as they have from time immemorial. *The Emperor Jones* turned out to be a fine collaboration, a strong piece of theater. Maestro Villa-Lobos conducted. It was a score for fifty instruments. It had a fantastic range of orchestral color and from delicate nocturnal fantasies, spectral visions, to crashing terrors and debacles. We rehearsed arduously, with tempos carefully discussed. When the heat was on, the dear man got lost to all but the force and power of his music, and we poor dancers had a time, let me assure you.

Arnold Schoenberg I never knew face to face, but we corresponded copiously. I wanted his permission to make a choreographic setting to his *Chamber Symphony No. 2*. My subject was the expulsion from the Garden of Eden of our legendary first parents. I outlined for him my ideas, especially the middle section of the work, where the two protagonists remember, in the midst of their misery, the joys of their lost paradise. I mentioned their innocence, their rapture in the radiant ambience of the garden, the symbolic temptation and their succumbing to it. Mr. Schoenberg answered me that it sounded quite interesting, but he insisted, most vehemently, that the work must contain nothing lewd, lascivious, salacious nor obscene. I promised faithfully that it would contain none of these dreadful things, and he gave me his permission. *The Exiles* turned out to be a good work. I have recently revived it for Sally Stackhouse and Louis Falco who have given it a brilliant performance.

Working with Norman Dello Joio, Gunther Schuller and Hugh Aitken has been very productive – I learned very much from them. One thing, especially, that a composer's work is finished. A choreographer's never. His work is always incomplete, and needs perpetual attention.

A few years ago, Juilliard gave Hindemith a festival of his works. I was assigned to do the choreography for his *The Demon*. Again there was much correspondence, this time transatlantic, since Herr Hindemith was in Germany. There was much discussion about the scenario and script of the ballet. I was dismayed by it. The ballet was first performed in 1924, and while the music still held up very well, the libretto was sadly outdated. No contemporary audience would have countenanced it. I proposed a new one, and after much negotiation and concessions on both sides, it was accepted. I began work with my dancers, and finally, Mr. Hindemith arrived. I had been warned by everyone that he was a most difficult man, testy, with a vile temper, a real prima donna, and that I'd better look out. As a matter of fact, he had warned me from Germany that he reserved the right of veto over my efforts. He sat out there where you are now, and we, in our tights and leotards, with a tape recording, performed the ballet from beginning to end. You may be sure that we were nervous. As the curtain fell on this preview, we heard a commotion out front. I was certain Mr. Hindemith was having an apoplectic seizure. It turned our that he was applauding and shouting his delighted approval. He hurried on stage and kissed all the girls and warmly congratulated Lucas Hoving and me. From then on, for the rehearsals and performances both here and in Washington, D. C., he insisted on conducting. He was a lamb. "You tell me, Mr. Limon, exactly what tempo you want. This is for the dance. The dance is the important thing." I wish I could tell you that the tempos were what we needed. But in any case, it was always a rare experience and a challenge, and never, never a dull moment. *The Demon* as a dance was not terribly good. My dancers and I gave it everything we had, but it was neither inspired nor inspiring. But it is a comfort to me that it delighted Mr. Hindemith.

The best thing, actually, is to have someone play and conduct for you, who has worked with you for years, for decades, and who knows you very well, and who is alert to your artistic virtues and defects, and who knows the dance completely. Such a person is my colleague, Simon Sadoff; who has gone with me to little out of the way places, and played the piano accompaniment, and to Europe, Latin America and the Orient, to conduct the great symphony orchestras for our dances in Buenos Aires and Tokyo. He can play, brilliantly, the Copland *Piano Sonata* for Doris Humphrey's *Day on Earth*. He can keep the dance, music and words perfectly timed and balanced in Norman Lloyd's *Lament for Ignacio Sanchez Mejias*. He can conduct the chorus and music in the *Missa Brevis* of Kodaly. Because you see, he is not only a brilliant musician and fine conductor, but he has become, over the years, also a dancer.

Simon Sadoff, conductor, pianist and musical director of the Limón Company, taking a bow with José Limón. Photo by Milton Oleaga. José Limón Dance Foundation Archives.

Mr. Kodaly was invited by the producer of National Education Television, Jac Venza, to view their film of my dance to his *Missa Brevis*. The dear man was very displeased. He didn't like it a bit. He said it was ugly, the choreography crude, the dancing worse, the costumes terrible. He had seen, he announced, Isadora Duncan dance in Budapest in 1911, and she was beautiful, lyrical, poetic, not like this ugliness. I was speechless. Martha Hill, who had accompanied me to this painful encounter, explained that this was a dance idiom and style indigenous to this country, and in consequence strange and jarring to one accustomed only to the European styles, that perhaps further experience and familiarity with contemporary dance styles would modify his opinion. After all, modern music had at first sounded crude and ugly. This she did with gentle tact and charm. Somewhat mollified, Mr. Kodaly turned to me and demanded to know why I did thus and so. Here, words failing him, he at eighty and some years of age, jumped from his seat, all five feet and some inches of him, his bright rosy cheeks flushed, his sky blue eyes flashing and white hair tossing, and danced before us an exasperated parody of what I had done on the screen. I was delighted. I wanted to call out "Bravo, Mr. Kodaly! If only I could do it like that, just like that!" Who can say that musicians are not dancers? We parted in a cordial mood – he even conceded that parts of the dance were not too unprepossessing. They were interesting, even impressive.

And so, dancer-musicians, musician-dancers, here you are on the threshold of the next half century which belongs to you. What music, what dances you will bring into the world! How privileged you are to be artists! You are that already, or you wouldn't be sitting here before me. Let me salute the puissance of your youth. You are young now, and now is forever. Youth is not wasted on the young: it comes at precisely the right moment. It is the only one you will ever have. It is your magic hour, verdant as spring, golden as sunrise. I adjure you to the courage and probity of the artist, to a terrible daring, to fortitude in the face of the challenge of nihilism, and lunatic horror. Some of you here will work with tradition. Others will find new roads. I hope the first will revere and conserve, but not embalm, the treasure of the past. There is a great difference between a pantheon and a mausoleum. The others, I hope, will not spit in the face of tradition. Remember the old girl is your mother, and there is a commandment, the fifth, if you will recall. Be truly a revolutionary, not a mere mutineer or rebel. Revolutions, after the ax and the guillotine and the firing squad have finished with their untidy work, can be glorious. Make yours one such. Remember you are peerless. Remember that art is redemptive, that your life will be half debacle, half apotheosis. You will be wounded. Wear your scars as the most exalted of decorations.

Reprinted from *The Juilliard Review Annual 1966–67* with permission of The Juilliard School and José Limón Dance Foundation.

3

THE DANCE HEROES OF JOSÉ LIMÓN

Norton Owen

The artistic life of José Limón was defined by heroes. Both his inspirations and his creations were painted with broad strokes on large canvasses. The first page of his autobiographical manuscript makes this point immediately in its style as well as in its content. "Late in the year nineteen hundred and twenty-nine I was born at No. 9 East 59th Street, New York City.

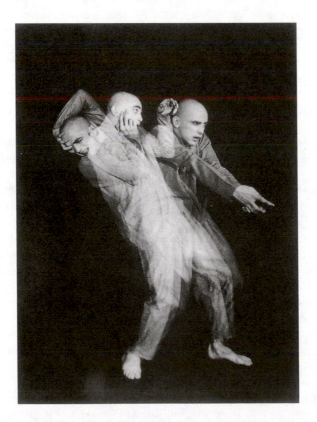

Harald Kreutzberg. Photo by Maurice Goldberg.
The Dance Collection, New York Public Library.

My parents were Isadora Duncan and Harald Kreutzberg. They were not present at my birth. I doubt that they were aware of their responsibility for my being. Presiding at my emergence into the world were two people who became my foster parents, Doris Humphrey and Charles Weidman. It was at their dance studio, in their classes, that I was born ... My grandparents were equally illustrious. They were Ruth St. Denis and Ted Shawn. All this constitutes an imposing pedigree, and with the exception of Harald Kreutzberg, an Austrian, a very American one."[1]

This passage cannot be taken literally, of course, but it demonstrates just how strongly Limón felt about the oversized personalities that shaped his point of view. The dance pioneers he credits as his ancestors were more than mere influences. Their personal styles were mirrored in the noble carriage and powerfull presence of Limón's persona, and the urgency of their dancing was invoked in many of Limón's stage works. It is this sense of determined individualism that distinguishes Limón's dances even now, more than a quarter-century after his death.

Limón's reach for the grand gesture seems to have predated his entry into the dance world, as evidenced by another passage in his autobiographical writings. Here he remembers leaving his adopted hometown of Los Angeles to seek fame as a painter in New York City. "I was talented. I was going to follow in the footsteps of Michelangelo, and every other inspired man who has ever wielded a paint brush, and made majestic beauty for his fellow men."[2]

Instead of remaining under the spell of the great painters, Limón saw a performance by Harald Kreutzberg in 1929 which immediately convinced him to pursue a dance career and led to his apprenticeship with Doris Humphrey and Charles Weidman. They became his family as well as his mentors, nurturing a fierce loyalty that became evident in 1938 when Martha Graham invited Limón to join her group. He was mightily tempted to do so, but events were again charted by his strong beliefs. "One does not abandon one's loyalties, no matter what. One does not live for gain, but for belief. I owed Doris Humphrey and Charles Weidman a debt. This obligation was concocted of archaic and highly unrealistic notions having to do with loyalty and honor."[3]

Limón often paid tribute to Doris Humphrey with such demonstrations of loyalty. He referred to her as "a genius"[4] and honored her with the unusual role of artistic director of his own company, but he did not often elaborate on the specific lessons learned at her feet. This makes a passage from one of his letters all the more meaningful as he describes seeing Humphrey's last performance, in a 1945 work called *Inquest* which portrayed her as a lame woman. Humphrey had choreographed the role for herself with her own considerable physical limitations in mind. Of *Inquest*, Limón wrote, "I am glad I saw her in this final vision.

I saw that life and art are in their very essence tragic, and for that reason noble and beautiful and exalted. I saw a confirmation of my goal. I did not want to entertain anyone, nor to be amusing. I wanted to do for people what Doris did for me that night. She gave me a vision of the beauty and majesty of tragedy."[5]

Soon after this incident, Limón began hitting his stride as a choreographer, incorporating the tragic majesty that he learned from Humphrey. Nowhere is this more apparent than in the title role of *The Moor's Pavane* (1949). Limón's embodiment of the tormented Othello shows us nobility gone wrong: the powerful but lonely leader who is conquered by a disloyal friend and his own inner turmoil. As Limón once commented in a program note, "Here is portrayed the tragedy of Everyman when he is caught in the pattern of tragic living."[6] Limón would later draw inspiration from another Shakespearean tragedy, *Macbeth*, in *Barren Sceptre*, a 1960 dance which had a short life.

The title role in *The Traitor* (1954) was modeled on Judas Iscariot and his betrayal of Jesus. Limón's own program note for this dance best summarizes the choreographer's intent. "The arch-betrayer, Judas Iscariot, is used in this work to symbolize all those tormented men who, loving too much, must hate; these men who, to our own day, must turn against their loyalties, friends and fatherlands, and, in some fearful cataclysm of the spirit, betray them to the enemy. This work, in its treatment, costuming and decor suggests our present era."[7]

This last sentence is a reference to Limón's inspiration for the work, the McCarthy hearings in which suspected Communists were asked to name names and turn against their own friends and colleagues. Limón originally created the title role of the tortured Judas for himself, though late in his life he would also perform the role of Christ (known as The Leader). In either case, Limón was clearly adept in reserving for himself roles that had the right mixture of grandeur and torment. These qualities were evidently present in his personal deportment as well as in his onstage portrayals. Walter Sorell once observed, "José Limón, a towering figure wrapped in the grandeur of lonesomeness, is an anachronism in our time, as Doris Humphrey once described him to me. José is a Baroque figure in this age of confusion through which he walks with Shakespeare and Bach on his mind, an Aztec prince at the mercy of a merciless and graceless world running amuck in a thicket of isms. ... He sings of the tormented soul in man."[8]

Such inner torment was brought to the surface in the title role of *The Emperor Jones* (1956), modeled after the Eugene O'Neill play concerning the leader of a slave revolution who is hunted by his own followers. Limón himself called this dance, "a symbolic synthesis of a man's disintegration through terror."[9] Perhaps Limón was also thinking of himself when he said of Brutus Jones that there was, "something not altogether ridiculous about his grandeur as he has a way of carrying it off."[10]

In the same year that he created *The Emperor Jones*, Limón explored related issues of the individual versus the group in *There is a Time*. All of the sections of this dance refer to the well-known biblical verses from Ecclesiastes which begin, "To every thing there is a season, and a time to every purpose under heaven."[11] In his original choreographic notes for the section entitled "A time to break down and a time to build up," he painted a dramatic picture of one man's potential influence over his peers. "Men form a segment of circle as though magnified – movements of dissolution, of breaking away from ordered pattern of circle each mutually repelled by his fellows and his place in the circle – convulsive and violent actions to secede – to get away. One figure can cause this breakdown, this dissolution. He can persuade or force others to defect. He can convince or persuade or force the slow or the unwilling – the revolutionary – the dissident – the heretic."[12]

Charles Weidman, Doris Humphrey and José Limón at Mills College, 1933.
José Limón Dance Foundation Archives.

A similar theme is seen in his notes for another section of the same dance, "A time to keep silence, and a time to speak," which was originally planned to have three men and three women in addition to the solo figures now featured. Of the silent female, Limón wrote, "This figure walks alone – austere and somber, wrapped in a cloak or mantle to distinguish it from three utterly frivolous couples who surround it and accost it with simian chatter and behavior – like a ground bass, grave and collected under a giddy superficial obligato. The lone figure maintains silence – despite the taunts, the mocking, the indignities heaped upon it by the others who are almost caricatures. Parody of theme – a degraded carnival – a festival of fools."[13] Limón goes on to describe the entrance of the solo male representing the counterpart to silence. "This man speaks perhaps when no one wishes to listen – he speaks earnestly and seriously and addresses his fellows who respond incredulously, then fearfully, then with resentment ... This speech is long overdue, or is prohibited, or is unpopular, or unwanted because it conveys an unpalatable truth."[14]

A parallel compositional structure can be seen in *Missa Brevis* (1958), a more formally abstract dance with dramatic undertones which pays tribute to the Polish people and their efforts to persevere after World War II. Limón danced the role of an unnamed solo figure who is characteristically set apart from the crowd. John Martin commented on the juxtaposition of the solos and group dances soon after the premiere. "His use of the group as a group is a natural outgrowth of the subject and the material; when the individual emerges he is nonetheless an individual, and when he takes his personal flashes of emotional realization back into the group he is no less a part of the group. There is a remarkable awareness of the solitude of the individual, and yet also of the group as something more than a mere aggregation of solitudes."[15]

Limón again grappled with the relationship between a solo figure and a group in *Psalm* (1967). Its premise was the ancient Jewish belief that all the world's sorrows rest upon thirty-six men. Limón distilled these thirty-six down to one, known as "The Burden Bearer," whose role was seen as an "outcast/martyr."[16]

While most of the heroes in Limón's dances were men, often conceived as vehicles for the choreographer, there were heroines as well. One little-known 1959 dance, *Tenebrae, 1914* was based on episodes in the life of Edith Cavell, the English nurse who was shot as a spy by the Germans in World War I. Cavell had aided wounded Allied soldiers, a courageous and noble act that fits the mold of other Limón heroes. The lead role was created for Ruth Currier, and Limón himself did not even appear in the dance. One review raved, "The startling realism and the searing relentless conclusion build to a cumulative dance-drama of tremendous impact."[17] In spite of this praise, the work exists today only on silent film and has not been performed in almost 40 years.

A better-known work created for Limón's female performers is *Dances for Isadora* (1971), choreographed near the end of his life in tribute to one of Limón's most profound inspirations. He had read Duncan's *My Life* soon after it was published in 1928, at about the same time when he was "reborn" as a dancer. In an issue of *Dance Perspectives* devoted to the legacies of Isadora Duncan and Ruth St. Denis, Limón wrote, "Although Isadora is my special inspiration, not one day of my thirty years as a dancer has gone by without one or the other, Duncan or St. Denis, poking me, inspiring me. Both women were profound humanists; one (Isadora) the great free spirit and the other (Miss Ruth) the theatrical genius of her day."[18]

Limón's final creation had another sort of heroine at its center. *Carlota* (1972) tells the story of the nineteenth century Belgian princess Carlota who became Empress of Mexico until her husband's assassination and her subsequent exile. The dance shows an older, insane Carlota who relives the earlier episodes of her life through a series of visions.

To list only Limón's successes when discussing his dance heroes might give the mistaken impression that there were no failures. Indeed there were, and they are equally valid demonstrations of Limón's philosophy. In his autobiography, he tells of what he learned from some of the forgotten Humphrey-Weidman works. "Heroic failure often carries with it a cathartic aftermath. One can find a somber solace in a superlative debacle. But how to endure living with a half-success, half-failure? With the knowledge that you failed to move, to transfigure, the spectator? That he left your performance untouched, unravished, merely lukewarm?"[19]

These lessons were put to the test in Limón's later years, when currents in the cultural world turned against him. In 1968, Don McDonagh severely criticized *Legend*, a Limón trio which attempted to explore the issue of slavery. "Mr. Limón, who is the grand old man by virtue of talent and tenure, has found himself increasingly at odds creatively with young choreographers' commitment to the abstract. It is a tidal shift, which Mr. Limón resists with Canute-like resolution."[20]

Limón had, in fact, made an important shift in his last decade, moving away from narrative dances and often presenting the dancers themselves as idealized beings in such large-scale works as *A Choreographic Offering* (1964) and *The Winged* (1966). One obvious reason for this was his involvement with The Juilliard School, where large groups of well-trained dancers were put at his disposal. Meanwhile, the composition of his own company had evolved from the strong and idiosyncratic personalities of Ruth Currier, Lucas Hoving, Betty Jones and Pauline Koner to a younger and more homogenous group.

And yet, even in his more abstract works of this period, such as *The Unsung* (1970), Limón put his unmistakable dramatic stamp on pure movement. One can get a feel for the atmosphere of *The Unsung* from Limón's description of its inspiration, an Indian tribal gathering where, "the dancers, baked in the sweat of exertion and fervor, danced under the merciless sun, moving as one, inscrutable, god-like, in perfect consonance with a pulse, a phrasing, an architecture of infinite complexity and subtlety, known only to them."[21]

In a *New York Times* profile published just weeks before Limón's death in 1972, Deborah Jowitt summed up both his persona and his position in the dance world at that time. "Within the dance he now seems like a king in exile from a foreign country. But a king, nonetheless."[22] Now that so many years have passed since Limón's death, we are able to view his contributions from a greater distance and appreciate the lasting impact of his many dance heroes. The question of exile is moot and his status as choreographic royalty is more evident than ever. Long live the king!

Notes

1. José Limón. unpublished autobiographical manuscript. p. 1.
2. Ibid., p. 34.
3. Ibid., p. 212.
4. Ibid., p. 63.
5. José Limón, letter to Pauline Koner, Betty Jones and Lucas Hoving, September 1, 1959.
6. José Limón, program note, ca. 1960.
7. José Limón, undated program note.
8. Walter Sorell, "Reviews: José Limón," Dance News, November 1972.
9. José Limón, quoted by Robert Bagar in program for premiere of *The Emperor Jones*, August 1956.
10. José Limón, concept notes for *The Emperor Jones*, 1956.
11. Ecclesiastes, Chapter 3, verse 1 (King James Version).
12. José Limón, concept notes for *There is a Time*, 1956.
13. Ibid.
14. Ibid.
15. John Martin, "José Limón's Tribute to the Human Spirit," *The New York Times*, May 18, 1958.
16. Lewis Segal, "José Limón Company at Bridges," *Los Angeles Times*, December 12, 1977.
17. Louis Horst, Dance Observer, August–September 1959.
18. José Limón, quoted by Walter Terry in *Dance Perspectives* 5, Winter 1960, p. 47.
19. Limón, autobiographical manuscript, p. 176.
20. Don McDonagh, "Limón Premiere in Dance Fete Finale," *The New York Times*, August 18, 1968.
21. José Limón, Opening Convocation Speech, American Dance Festival, July 8, 1963.
22. Deborah Jowitt, "Limón Pursues His Visions," *The New York Times*, October 8, 1972.

4

PAULINA REGINA

Charles D. Tomlinson

In 1960 I came to New York from London where I had been studying and
working, hoping to get a fresh start in my own country as a scenic and
costume designer. I took all sorts of jobs in the theater in an effort to
make every possible connection. I assisted other designers, stage managed, house managed, acted in several plays and even landed a dancing
role in the short-lived musical *Tiger Rag.* Although thinly spread, I didn't
want to miss a thing. Included in my busy schedule were classes with
David Wynne, a Limón dancer. Some years earlier I had studied dance
in college with Foster Fitz-Simmons (who had been a member of the
Denishawn Company) and for four years had performed in summer theater productions and for a brief stint in New York. My major course of
study at university was theater with a fellowship in both scenic and costume design. That was and is my first love. My second love still is the
dance, specifically the dancing of José Limón.

It was in the spring of 1960 that I learned from David that the José
Limón Dance Company was going to tour Central and South America. It
struck my fancy to ask for the job of maintaining the wardrobe. The
prospect of working and traveling with such an outstanding company
would certainly be exciting and seeing that part of the world might be a
once-in-a-lifetime experience.

The first time I saw the company perform was in London at the Sadler's
Wells Theatre in 1957; I was totally mesmerized by the experience.
I rushed backstage after the final curtain to express my thanks and share
my excitement. To my surprise, I met Mr. Limón himself. "I would love
to design for your company some day" I stammered, surprising myself
as I spoke. He was most gracious and made no promises but suggested
that if I ever came to New York to work I might give him a call. The
chance seemed remote since at the time I was designing scenery for a
series of television plays in London and had no plans to return to
America or to settle in New York.

Three years later, in New York, I decided to follow the lead David had
given me. I would pursue the job It would be a way to become affiliated
with the company that I so much admired. My long-held dream was to

design for the Limón company and later on I might have a chance to do so. I was hell bent on trying. Oh! The tenacity of youth.

After a rather stern interview with Mrs. Limón, she directed me to speak further with Tom Skelton, the company's lighting designer and production stage manager. Having passed muster with both these formidable people, I had a job for the summer and the following autumn. First came the American Dance Festival in New London, Connecticut and then the tour of Central and South America, including two cities in Mexico. This was the beginning of an association that would spawn some of the happiest and most creative times of my life. I continued to manage the wardrobe for the next thirteen years. There was a period of several years before I began to design for the company. It was a time of testing.

I began at the true beginning by washing tights and assisting Nellie Hatfield, who had returned for another summer of collaborating with Pauline in building and repairing the company costumes. I was in the presence of two true professionals, both old enough to be my mother. That summer they were working on another task: the construction and repairs for the costumes in readiness for the tour. I pitched in to do my part, often feeling like the "green kid" in their company; however, I soon found my niche and set about doing the many tasks at hand. All of this took place in the basement of Palmer Auditorium during the American Dance Festival (ADF).

As the company was completing performances, I was busy cleaning, organizing and packing all of the costumes, shoes, tights, sewing notions, extra fabrics for replacements, shoe dyes, elastics and just about everything you could think of for emergencies, in preparation for the tour. I also made an inventory of every item as I packed. We carried a second set of costumes for every dance in the event of unforeseen disasters. I even brought along my new portable Singer sewing machine and a miraculous transformer, provided by Tom Skelton, which could adapt local amps and volts to power that the machine could use. It was a good thing since there were numerous times when major repairs were needed.

I was nearing the completion of my pre-packing activities. The four walls were lined with great orange fiberglass packing containers capable of being dropped by parachute at any destination should the necessity arise. Thankfully, it didn't. Our equipment was loaded and unloaded in the usual fashion.

Pauline came down to see how things were progressing. Although she seemed pleased with what she saw, she began taking things from one packing case and putting them in another. She did it several times and I made quick mental notes so that I could adjust my inventory to match her changes. After a bit, I questioned her motives and was roundly told that it would be best to do things her way and that I could change them to suit myself after we got to South America. I suggested that I had not come there to learn to do my job and thought that my organization might best be left as it was. To this day I am not sure where I found the nerve to say that. Clearly she was not ready to relinquish what had been her responsibility; this would take some time to accomplish.

Before there was time to speak further, Martha Hill, a friend and Director of the Dance Division of the Juilliard School in New York and also a founder of the ADF, and José arrived at the bottom of the stairs. They beckoned Pauline to join them for their customary gin and tonic. An hour or so later, as I was about to leave for supper, the Trio returned to the costume room. Pauline called to me in a mellow and most reassuring tone of voice and directed me to work in my own fashion. I suspect that this change of heart in giving in to my method was a simple warning to me that I had better get it right, whatever it was that I was doing. Pauline had always been in total charge before so it was a new experience for her to hand over the reins of the wardrobe to me. As the tour got underway, things relating to the costumes ran smoothly. Pauline accepted my efforts and left the day to day responsibilities to me. It was a brand new role for her and she soon softened her scrutiny and relaxed in the assurance that all would be well. I believe that she felt that she had found a true compatriot in me and from that realization grew our long friendship.

Early one morning, on arriving at the theater in Quito, Equador, the day after our first performance, she saw that I had washed José's maroon velvet robe which he wore in *The Moor's Pavane* and hung it out to dry in the tropical sun. She had never heard of such a thing as washing velvet and was certain that I had ruined it. She was not at all pleased and for a moment I thought that I might be on the next plane headed north. With no little effort I explained my actions. The costume had been made no wetter with water than when it had come off José's body; the only difference being that I had run cold water and mild soap through the garment in an effort to freshen and help preserve it. She was extremely dubious until she saw the costume back on José and realized that it both looked and smelled better. At first Pauline found not being involved somewhat difficult and often asked if there wasn't some way that she could help. She continued to be interested. For the first time in thirty-two years she didn't have to concern herself with maintaining costumes. Involving herself in anything and everything to do with company activities had always been her major concern. Now there was one less thing on her agenda.

In truth, as the company grew and prospered, other responsibilities had been handed over to others. Thomas Skelton became Production Stage

Manager and later Lighting Designer. Susan Pimsler took on the job of
booking agent and arranged all transportation both nationally and internationally. Conductor and musical arranger Simon Sadoff took charge of
all things musical. By 1960 much that had been Pauline's domain fell into
other hands. I believe that she began enjoying being Mrs. José Limón
without having to work as hard as she had done for so many years. From
the beginning of José's company, she managed the budget, paid the
bills, arranged bookings and transportation, drew up contracts and
attended to the payroll just as she had done for the Humphrey-Weidman
Company. Simply put, she felt that her role was to relieve José of responsibilities, leaving him free to make dances. Her job was defined as doing
whatever it took *to be there* for the José Limón Dance Company.

Since the formation of the Humphrey-Weidman Company in 1928,
Pauline's sense of overall responsibility had been the same. Pauline
Lawrence first met Doris Humphrey and Charles Weidman at the
Denishawn School in Los Angeles. She was just out of high school, could
play the piano and came to the school as a rehearsal accompanist. The
year was 1917. She discovered dance, art, theater and beauty all at that
moment. It set the compass for the rest of her life. Her mission was to
facilitate the art of making dances. She never wavered. During her later
years with Denishawn, Pauline was coerced into a costume and put on
stage. I have found no reviews of her performance, but I suspect she
showed herself to be up to the task. There was never a doubt in her
mind; what was to be done, had to be done. Simply put, she would do it.

Later on, in 1927, after Doris Humphrey and Charles Weidman left the
Denishawn company, her participation provided the underlying structure
for the Humphrey-Weidman Company and school in New York City.
Pauline's responsibilities were formidable, but she still found the energy
to run the little communal household as well: a group consisting of herself, Doris and Charles and later on José and Peter Hamilton, a member of
the Humphrey-Weidman Company. This meant cooking and shopping as
well as seeing that all the bills were paid. Pauline's stamina and dedication under those conditions were truly heroic. Years later she turned her
support to the dreams and needs of José's company. By that time she had
become Mrs. Limón. That occurred on October 13, 1941, in San Francisco.

In 1945 when Doris was no longer able to dance and maintain her
company, it was Pauline who proposed that she become Artistic Director
of José's company. This turn of events brought Doris out of her depression and helped set the course for the fledgling Limón company. She
could resume choreographing with dancers she knew, many of whom
she had taught. She could also assist and encourage José as he began
building a repertory of works for his company. It proved to be an
inspired and productive collaboration.

As a designer, Pauline did not work through her ideas with drawing or sketching. (The existing sketches were done by José.) She created by using elements from photos and illustrations which she collected. She possessed a fair assortment of art and costume reference books from which to cull ideas. She also knew fashion and accumulated a large collection of illustrations from newspapers and magazines. Armed with an assortment of pictures, she simply relied on her own good taste in selecting what she thought was suitable. A little of this and a lot of that – it usually worked. Chief among her gifts was her remarkable intuition. Of course everything she created was not perfect, but it was tasteful and it worked. There were times when she would change her mind and start over. Other times she returned to previously designed costumes and changed them just for a fresher look. I think it a fair assessment to say that her designs were subtle but suitable.

Pauline had a remarkably gifted helper in Nellie Hatfield who brought great skills and an abundance of patience to the creative process. The two ladies were an amazing team. Mrs. Hatfield would listen to Pauline's ideas, look at her references and produce anything she was called on to create. There was no aspect of cutting, sewing or finishing a costume of which she was incapable. She understood Pauline's signs and signals and was a craftsman with acute sensitivity and artistic integrity. Not only were the costumes beautifully designed, they were made to couturier specifications. Mrs. Hatfield eventually retired to her home and family in Brooklyn as aging brought on sight problems and her energies diminished. It was a sad time for Pauline and me and a turning point for the company.

Not long after Mrs. Hatfield's retirement, Pauline turned briefly to the giant New York house of Brooks-Van Horn for costume construction. This was not a good match. Brooks was accustomed to firm facts, tight sketches and assembly line tactics. Pauline simply didn't work that way. They soon parted company on grounds of incompatibility.

Fortunately a woman named Betty Williams was running a small but good costume shop downtown on West 14th Street where she catered mostly to Off-Broadway theater productions. The atmosphere at her shop was very much "hands-on" and a designer could easily guide the development of ideas into garments. Betty's shop became the workroom for the company's costumes for a long time to follow.

There are many ways a designer can create. It is not unusual to work right on the body of the performer and develop the costume in phases as the dance develops. The dancer, the movement and the costume must become one. Surprisingly, Pauline's costumes were created independently from the dancers; yet, they became an integral part of the movement.

When Pauline's costumes did not please her or serve the dance well her efforts would be reappraised and new ideas developed. On other

Pauline Lawrence Limón and José Limón seated in the studio of their house in New Jersey. The Dance Collection, New York Public Library.

occasions work would continue until completion but with an eye to making changes later, if and when the dance proved beneficial to the repertory. Odd as it may seem, the less successful the dance, the less successful the costumes. It was rather like hand-in-hand suicide. A good example of this happening was José's dance *My Son, My Enemy*, created at the ADF as a dramatic conflict set in Zsarist Russia. He, Louis Falco and the company thrashed through many a conflict but to little effect. Costume solutions seemed to evaporate as we pushed toward some conclusion. After the dance premiered, Pauline and I packed away the costumes forever. I had co-designed them so it was a sad beginning for me.

There was a period toward the end of her career when Pauline relied more on simple, unadorned line and color for her creations. One of my earliest memories was her decision to replace her handsome costumes for Doris' *Passacaglia* with leotards and tights. The change certainly revealed the dancers' body lines but did little to increase the appeal of the dance itself. I think Pauline wanted to try it for the sake of change. Soon after, the piece was dropped from the repertory.

There were other dances which relied solely on the supplier of tights and leotards, Capezio's. *A Choreographic Offering* and *The Winged* were both dressed in leotards and tights, not, I suspect solely for economic reasons. Each dance had it's own unique palette of colors. As Pauline's collaborator on both these projects and master of the dye pots, I had fingers, hands and arms dyed to match the costumes for days after the opening nights.

A work created for the company in 1953 by Doris Humphrey was called *Ritmo Jondo*. For this dance, Pauline created a stunning set of costumes in black and white. She relied on Spanish and Basque influences to create long black skirts of sunburst pleated faille in the flamenco style with dropped waists for the four women, with white cotton and lace peasant blouses. The men looked handsome in white shirts with full, long-sleeves and open at the neck. Their costumes had black woolen knee breeches with white knee socks overlaced with black thongs. Black hats completed the picture. Scarves which the women used were flung with abandon. The dance was concerned with passions and the movement of the costumes complimented this mood. The whole look was sophisticated. The dance and the costumes were greeted with great acclaim.

The costume ideas for *La Malinche* seem to have come from sketches made by José based on Mexican peasant clothes. Pauline took them to stunning realization, clothing the two men (José and Lucas Hoving) in white cotton broadcloth and Pauline Koner (for her role as La Malinche) in a peasant-like full-skirted dress and with a heavy, gold-trimmed, black, stiff overskirt for her second role in the dance as the Conquistador's mistress.

It was by default, or more specifically the result of an ongoing dissatisfaction with the costumes designed by Ming Cho Lee, to augment his monumental and beautiful "gothic ruin" setting for *Missa Brevis*, that brought Pauline to create her altogether fitting, somber-toned, peasant-like costumes for this dance. She worked in shades of gray, blue and black, touched with amber, lavender and brown. What she achieved with José was an ocean of almost monochromatic, moving figures bound together in their sorrow and hope. The costumes' contribution here was pivotal to the emotional effect of the dance.

To better appreciate some of Pauline's most successful and vivid creations for the Limón company, one should consider *The Traitor*. The rich, deep colors of stained glass were her inspiration. Short, boxy velour vests gave bulk to the men's chests. High-wasted pants, also of velour, brought gravity to the dancers' silhouette. Silk shirts with full-cut bloused sleeves completed the costumes, evoking the image of nineteenth century Dutchmen. The costumes, were, nevertheless, of no specific style or period. It was a unique and serenely beautiful way to dress the story of Christ's betrayal. Pure inspiration.

For a work by Doris Humphrey created in 1951, *Night Spell*, Pauline used gossamer nylon fabric over nude-colored leotards, enhancing the other-worldliness of the three apparitions which seemed to float and vaporize as they surrounded José in his torment of the night. With imaginative lighting enriching the stage picture, the four dancers created true magic.

When designing costumes for *The Moor's Pavane* Pauline found her sources for Desdemona and Emilia in a German costume history book. She relied solely on these drawings for the silhouette and detail, giving all her attention to the selection of the colors and fabrics to achieve the effects she wanted. The complicated underskirts for the women were her own invention. Sources for the other two costumes (The Moor and His Friend) are unknown to me but it is clear that she stayed with the high renaissance for inspiration. I suspect that her choice of thick, ribbed woolen knee socks for Lucas' costume was an invention to simulate soft, high leather boots appropriate to the period that were not possible within the budget. It is also possible that the choice was simply to give Lucas wider calves. In several instances, ballet companies around the world who have taken *The Moor's Pavane* into their repertories have chosen to make the change from long socks to boots for the role of Iago. I suspect that Pauline would not reject the adjustment. This dance is considered by many to be José's most eloquent masterpiece and Pauline's handsome costumes are undoubtedly the crowning touch. *The Moor's Pavane* was performed at the White House at the request of President and Mrs. Johnson on the occasion of the state visit of King Hussein of Jordan in 1967. The white lace handkerchief used in the performance is now part of the permanent collection at the Johnson Library in Austin, Texas.

In my opinion, Pauline created her finest, most beautiful and ingenious costumes for *There is a Time*. Here she most perfectly complemented the choreography, which has the structure of a theme and variations. The narrative structure of *There is a Time* comes from the biblical book of Ecclesiastes: There is a time to be born, to die, to embrace, to sow, to reap, to kill, to heal, to speak and to be silent, to dance, etc. As each section of the dance evolves from the previous section, the number of dancers and their formations change. With no less effectiveness, the ways that the costumes are worn subtly change as well in perfect accompaniment.

The women's dresses are of beige jersey, full skirted (a circle and a half) and reach to the floor. The matching bodices are fitted with long sleeves. The sleeves are sometimes worn short by collecting them at the upper arms with an internal drawstring. At times, the necks of the bodices are open; at other times closed. There are also full, knife-pleated, organdy skirts in various pastel colors which are worn both under the beige skirts and over them. The men wear beige, tan, or brown woolen jersey, fitted knee breeches. Their full-bodied shirts are of beige jersey matching the women's dresses. They also have sleeveless jackets (opening in front) of tan, dusty brown and pale pumpkin. They perform with and without their jackets and with shirt sleeves worn long or drawn up toward the shoulder (as the women do). All the changes are distinctive, effective and subtle.

Pauline undoubtedly spent many hours at rehearsals making suggestions on the ways that the costumes could be adjusted and worn in each section. The versatility of her designs could come only from years of experience and her acutely developed sensibility to both the dancers and the spirit of the choreography.

As Pauline's health began to fail in 1968, she took a less active role in company activities, but her ardent interest never flagged. The modern dance to which she had devoted most of her life achieved glorious fruition in José's company. Undoubtedly, Pauline was a significant influence in José's life and in his work. When she first met him at the Humphrey-Weidman school in 1928, she said that he would be the man in her life. He certainly was.

I was indeed fortunate to have been taken into Pauline's confidence after our shaky beginning. Suffice to say that I count it among my major achievements that I was. My work and collaboration for so many years with her and José remains a promontory from which I view the remainder of my work.

My friendship with José and Pauline developed into a deep and abiding love. As fate would decree it, it was I who was with each of them as they drew their last breaths. The sadness that this brought can only be compared to the loss of my own dear parents. The Limóns had not unwittingly become my "mentor" parents.

5

VOICES OF THE BODY

Betty Jones

In 1947 I joined the José Limón Dance Company after having met José at Jacob's Pillow in the Berkshires a few years earlier. Within the first year of joining the company, José asked if I would teach a beginners' class at the Dance Players Studio on West 56th Street in Manhattan where he was teaching and rehearsing the company. This was a start of a long journey performing and teaching for twenty-three years with the José Limón Dance Company. A series of teaching venues developed for me first at The American Dance Festival, in New London, Connecticut, and later at ADF when it had moved to North Carolina. I also taught the Limón technique at The Juilliard School, where in 1951 a new dance division was created by Martha Hill which incorporated the techniques of Limón as well as Martha Graham and classical ballet. In 1958 Dr. Lulu Sweigard also joined The Juilliard faculty and introduced teaching labs and a class called "Anatomy for Dancers". After observing her classes for a year, I began to realize that some of the movement vocabulary that I was teaching conflicted with principles of anatomically correct body mechanics. If done often it could be harmful to the dancer. Eventually, I had the good fortune to assist Dr. Sweigard for thirteen years at The Juilliard School. This association was valuable in helping me gain a deeper and more thorough understanding of the skeletal weight – supporting structure and it's joints, as well as good body balance resulting in more efficient movement and a better coordination of the muscles. Dr. Sweigard often worked with images which I found very helpful in freeing my own body and gradually I started incorporating these images and principles into my own teaching of Limón techniques. On our endless bus rides during the Limón Company tours, I would have long discussions with José on this subject. They were a cause of much humor and amusement between us. He was passionate about movement, dance, Chopin, Bach and Michelangelo, whereas anatomy or Laban's ideas about effort/shape hardly tickled his fancy. Yet he was concerned that the technique classes would prepare the dancers for the demands of his choreography both technically and stylistically. Before going further, I must explain that the Limón technique is not codified.

Many years ago, a Dutch woman who was studying at ADF when I was teaching there asked me to come to Holland and establish a syllabus for the Limón technique to be followed in her school. I spoke to José about this, and his answer was no. He felt that the idea of a rigid outline would limit the possibilities and would establish a structure that would confine and constrict the creativity that was inherent in the technique. All of José's teaching was aimed at helping us find our own way of moving, to unearth or discover our uniqueness.

With any discussion of the technique which José established as the basis of his classes, one cannot start without first talking of Doris Humphrey. José started his formal dance training in New York with Doris Humphrey and Charles Weidman at the school they founded in the early thirties. It was there that José first encountered the ideas which became central to his philosophy. The quality of the body's weight was vitally important in Humphrey's approach and the vocabulary of her technique incorporated what she referred to as "the arc between two deaths" or, simply put, a fall and rebound. This idea was profoundly important to José and became a cornerstone of his technique, along with her discovery of the vocabulary of suspension and succession. This philosophy was deeply embedded in José's body. I want to quote Doris's declaration: "I wish my dance to reflect some experience of my own in relationship to the outside world; to be based on reality illumined by imagination; to be organic rather than synthetic; to call forth a definite reaction from my audience; and to make its contribution toward the drama of life." These ideas were reflected in José's classes, and his movement phrases were passionate, gorgeous, full of strong movement which swept through space.

José said "The modern idiom has extended the range of expressive movement and communicative gesture tremendously. The modern dancer strives for a complete use of the body as his instrument". To this end he used isolated parts of the body to "speak" with individual qualities and referred to this idea as "voices of the body".

The exploration of movement possibilities of various parts of the body was a way for dancers to experiment and find their own voices, their own unique qualities of expression. Let's take the shoulder as an example. By rotating it forward or backward or lifting and dropping it and using those motions to motivate a turn, a jump, or a fall, a dancer could "speak" through that shoulder, not just move it, but use the shoulder as a voice with a motivation behind it. Jose also liked to refer to the body as being like an orchestra, with perhaps the hips being a bass drum and the shoulders a piccolo. The combination of movements of various parts of the body is infinite, and the exploration lends itself to movement rich in dynamic rhythms, bringing contrasting movement qualities between the upper and lower body.

Sometimes José would ask the accompanist to play middle C on the piano, and after we had listened to the purity of that sound, he would ask the pianist to play the same note with the elbow, José used this example for students to illustrate how a movement can be articulated clearly or poorly. He encouraged them always to strive for simplicity and clarity without extraneous movement, superfluous energy or unwanted tension that would interfere with the original intent.

The use of arms and hands were particularly important to José. By reaching, pushing, receiving or grasping, gestures of the arms and hands could communicate volumes. One could convey a radiating warmth from curved arms embracing space or a fierce defiance by the slash of an elbow. We spent class time just articulating the hands in a way that was similar to Doris' hands study, pushing forward with the heel of the hand opening the palm and fingers, followed by a release and a slight contraction at the knuckles returning the hands close to the chest. The hands and arms were never static, but breathing and speaking, trained to reflect movement starting from the center of the body. Gestures of the legs were not used as purely decorative elements, but rather as an integral part of the motivation of movement. José used arms and legs as an extension and reflection of what was happening in the torso and pelvis.

He also spoke as a painter comparing space to a canvas on which we must paint with daring strokes. In technique class José taught a long, low walk, on which he superimposed a contracted torso, arms and fists, which slowly unfolded and opened into a full extension of the spine, arms and hands. The legs maintained their steady, driving force through space. This movement had to be felt from one's being, finding the inner truth for one's self. It was not without reason that on the company's first trip to Paris we visited the Rodin Museum. According to the great sculptor Auguste Rodin, "the body always expresses the spirit for which it is the shell". The body always speaks, perhaps eloquently or perhaps without meaning, but never without telling us a great deal about the condition and thoughts of the individual.

The Limón technique emphasizes and utilizes movement within the chest like the ebb and flow of the ocean. In this technique the chest constantly expands and retreats. This doesn't mean the chest literally retreats, but softens, relaxes and becomes more vulnerable. The part of the body containing emotion, as Delsarte pointed out, is in the chest, and we explored an infinite range of emotional possibilities through articulations within that part of the body. Arms and hands are directly involved and extend and describe more fully the quality and motion within the chest, which renders the human language universally comprehensible.

Other trademarks of the technique are Limon's inward and outward rotations of the knee. These rotations in front, to the side and back of the body were movement explorations which he frequently developed as an impetus for balances, turns and jumps. Similarly, the movement of the hips forward and backward, laterally or rotating and circling in space were the basis for extended phrases across the dance floor. These were not set studies, but a wealth of ideas to be used to move us through space and train us to a higher body intelligence. José most often composed a phrase for class on the spur of the moment, experimenting, trying this way and that. Gradually he would let the timing and counts evolve as the phrase clarified itself. He seldom did the same thing twice and one time I had the nerve to ask which way he wanted it. "Just do it, Betty." When someone got the hang of a phrase he would say "do it like so and so."

In teaching the technique over the years, I have utilized many of the principles spoken of here. Of the elements I have not touched upon, but which was one of the activities in José's technique classes often introduced at the beginning of class was the combination of a swing of the torso used in conjunction with a swing of the arms and a deep quick drop into a plié and a slower recovery. This movement fits well into 3 counts: one count for the drop, and two counts for the recovery and suspension. A suspension is the change of direction when the body, in that soaring, effortless magical moment after moving away from the gravitational pull, is slowly being reclaimed by it.

After a few successional movements and slow passive stretches I like to start a class with head swings, adding some chest, and then more body with arms, maintaining the emphasis on fall and suspension. The letting go of weight is difficult and most everyone struggles with it, but once one has found the way to truly give in to gravity, one is well on the way to conquering the technique. For leg swings, it is important to locate the hip joint (or thigh joint as Dr. Sweigard preferred to call it) in order to gain a freer swing. Afterwards, inward and outward rotation can be added.

The subject of rhythm I believe to be the most difficult and elusive. Each movement has a fullness and rhythm of its own, with specific dynamic characteristics which occur because of the ideas to be expressed. When a movement phrase is being refined by exploring possibilities of dynamics, energy levels, suspensions and giving in to the gravitational pull, a rhythmic structure starts to establish itself. The use of interchanging even and uneven meters and intricate syncopations are frequently foreign to beginning dancers who are usually more comfortable with steady 4/4 or 3/4 meter most often encountered in popular music. José enjoyed dividing four quarter notes into eight eighth notes which he phrased as counts of three, three, and two. This then was used in many ways, perhaps starting with a walk in four counts, and piqués in a square with the three, three, two.

Last year, Fritz Ludin, my husband and partner, and I were teaching a workshop in Lyon, France at the Centre International de la Danse, focusing on the essence of Limón quality, and how to escape the confinement of a 4/4 meter. Most students composed phrases to fit meters close to their hearts, but when examined carefully, often their movements needed extra counts to be complete. Rhythm and counts changed immensely, and phrases ended up with odd counts which added a vibrancy that was very exciting.

In *There is a Time* created by José in 1956, he emphasized the two opposite qualities of rhythm: metric and breath rhythm. The duet *A Time to Speak, A Time to Keep Silence* is choreographed without traditional musical accompaniment. It uses clapping sounds for the man's solo, which has driving, rhythmic, beating steps, uneven in timing and using phrases in counts of 5's and 7's. The woman's part, which alternates with the man's solo and signifies the silence of the sectional title, *A Time to Keep Silence*, is in complete contrast to the man's dance. It gently repeats her phrases, without any counts, always varying her timing using what we call breath rhythm. The juxtaposition of the two rhythms is dynamic, giving great contrast and emphasizing the difference in the attitude of the two dancers.

My interest in rhythm and dynamics of other dance cultures started while touring with the José Limón Dance Company twice to South America and once to Europe and Asia. These tours were the beginning of new connections and cultural exchanges with the international dance community. In 1963 when the company performed in Japan. José was instrumental in securing fellowships for some young Japanese dancers to study at The Juilliard School. In the seventy's Fritz and I helped introduce dance students and dancers in France to the technique of José Limón. Charles and Stephanie Reinhart, directors of the current American Dance Festival where I have had the pleasure of teaching students and young professionals from around the globe, have expanded the festival to foreign countries. These assignments have taken me to India, China, Japan, Korea, Indonesia and Russia. I feel a deep satisfaction in sharing my dance and teaching experiences and the heritage of José Limón, Doris Humphrey and Dr. Lulu Sweigard. In Moscow, exquisite dancers from the Moiseyev Dance Company brought their dance temperament to class and infected everyone with their explosive enthusiasms. In Guangzhou, China, working from dawn to late afternoon with the Guangdong Modern Dance Company, China's first official modern dance company, I was impressed by the daring style of the dancers' choreography. I saw wonderful pieces in which they communicated their experiences of growing up in China and revealing much about Chinese culture and China's history. I could hear in the back of my

Betty Jones with student at Théâtre Contemporain de la Danse, Paris.
Photo copyright Marion-Valentine. Collection of Betty Jones.

mind José say, BRAVO! And I'm sure we were in total agreement that it was a privilege to teach them technique, good body mechanics and to encourage them to develop their own modern dance rooted in their own culture.

Fritz and I went to St. Petersburg in 1990 to reconstruct *There is a Time* for the Maly Opera Ballet Company. This was the first time any Russian company had performed a modern dance choreographed by an American. The dancers were required to take a modern dance class before their rehearsals with us. There was fear and consternation at first at not having their daily ballet class, but after a few days the dancers relaxed, and were performing their evening ballet performances with more freedom, much to their surprise. We spent a month with them, and by the time the dancers premiered the work we were proud to think that they had really taken hold of the movement of José's beautiful work. The result was wonderful. Local audiences from St. Petersburg and Moscow, including many artists, filled the Imperial Theater and were enthralled with the dancers' performance.

In recent years there has been a resurgence of Limón technique in Europe. Today's dancers and students are well versed in contact improvisation and release techniques, approaches that find inspiration in free vigorous movements, including off balance movements and gliding on to and away from the floor. Limón technique also has a daring and a falling through space which shares this aspect of Dionysian passion. I believe the technique has survived and is in demand all over the world mainly because of its lack of strict, codified movements. It leaves enough space for teachers and students alike to find their own way, and to be creative in their use of the technique. We've come a long way from the perfectly centered dancers, the Apollonian (which José was always talking about) to the Dionysian, that not only inspired him but which he also advocated in his teaching.

6

MY DANCE FAMILY

Charles H. Woodford

The door to the living room at the end of the long, dark hallway which connected the rooms of our apartment, was shut, but the groaning bass and tweedling treble coming from within meant that José was alone at his peddle-powered organ, immersed in Bach. He was not to be disturbed. Nor was he to be disturbed when he was sleeping, which seemed to be a great deal of the time.

It was my mother's (Doris Humphrey) idea that the principals of the Humphrey-Weidman Company live in this seven-room, floor-through flat on the fifth floor at Thirty-One West Tenth Street. It was a way of economizing during the Depression. Today, I suppose, you would call it a commune, but then it was simply my family. José Limón and I were the youngest, though separated by twenty-five years. The rest of the family consisted of my mother, Charles Weidman, my seafaring father Charles F. Woodford, my German governess Marga Hein, Pauline Lawrence (eventually to become Pauline Limón), the cook/housekeepers Hermine and Susan (when times were good), and various dancers, friends and relatives in need of a place to stay. My baby-talk mispronunciation of José and Pauline as "E" and "Pumba" became their nicknames within the household.

Our living room faced old New York, a row of stately brownstone townhouses from the nineteenth century. An organ grinder with a monkey would sometimes play *Sidewalks of New York* or *My Wild Irish Rose*, and I would throw pennies to him. When the fruit and vegetable man was sighted coming down the street with his horse-drawn cart, Marga or Hermine would scurry down to buy whatever was to be on the menu that night. My room, at the rear of the apartment, had a view of the Empire State Building, called the "The Empty State Building" because of its high vacancy rate. The staccato of jackhammers resounded throughout the neighborhood from early morning to late at night as the Sixth Avenue Elevated was torn down and replaced by the Sixth Avenue Subway. I was told that the scrap metal was being sold to the Japanese and would be coming back at us in the form of ammunition before long.

Left to right: Charles Weidman, Doris Humphrey, José Limón and house guest
Pauline Chellis; Charles Humphrey Woodford in foreground. Blairstown, New Jersey.
Collection of Charles Humphrey Woodford.

José and Charles Weidman owned a country property near Blairstown,
New Jersey, "the farm," where we all went on weekends and during the
parts of the summer that were not spent at Bennington College. At first
the place had no electricity, and water was supplied by a gasoline pump.
To get the pump going when the family arrived, Charles and José would
go up the hill to the pump house with clubs in hand to kill any

rattlesnakes lurking there. For years, rattlesnake tails hung on the kitchen wall as momentoes of these forays.

The bedrooms were named for colors. José lived in the Blue Room, painted a deep cobalt; my mother stayed in the mint-colored Green Room; and Pauline (or sometimes Marga) and I shared the Red Room, so-called because of its red curtains and spreads. Charles had the bow-windowed, antique pine-paneled master bedroom. The rest of the Company members and friends would sleep on the sofa, in an attic room, or in the garçonniere cabin attached to the barn.

In an atmosphere that was part work-party and part house-party, the men built walls, patios, and a tool house of stone and cement. The women kept house and did most of the cooking. Everyone helped to tend the gardens. Perhaps inspired by the example of Jacob's Pillow, Charles installed a dance studio in the barn. He also hoped that the barn would eventually house dormitories, although that dream was to go unrealized. The sweat of physical labor was balanced by the sweat of creative work in the barn. The choreography and studies that were created there on weekends found their way to the Humphrey-Weidman Studio in New York during the week.

For recreation my mother liked to work with her hand loom, and there were always outdoor games such as badminton and catch. There were also long cocktail hours on the front porch overlooking the expanse of fields, woods, hills, and a toy train chugging and hooting three miles away. As daylight dimmed, oil lamps were lit, and conversations became hilarious.

On rainy afternoons or after dinner, Charles liked to organize long sessions of "Racing the Devil," a kind of solitaire in which as many players as possible each had a deck of cards which they would run around the table to play. My mother did not participate because it involved gambling even though the stakes were only pennies. Another popular game was Hide-in-the-Dark, a variation of hide-and-seek in which players crowded together in a cramped space with all the lights out. I longed to play, but was forbidden on the grounds that the game took place long after my bedtime. I think my denial also had something to do with the fact that it was considered slightly risqué. No one was ever up very early in the morning except me; I was cautioned to be quiet. I usually spent those early hours in the attic pouring over *Look* and *Life* magazines, which showed photos of disasters such as the Japanese War in China and the effect of various sizes of bombs on buildings.

Holidays often centered around me as the child of the family. One Easter Sunday Pauline told me to hurry outside to see the marshmallow tree which had sprouted in her garden. There I found a spindly sapling that had magically grown marshmallows at the tips of its branches. Back in New York on Halloween, Charles and José rigged a cardboard skeleton to my door with invisible thread. When I opened the door, I saw a skeleton dancing in the middle of the floor. They roared with laughter as I stood petrified. Christmas was an important affair for everyone in the family with real candles on the tree which were lit for about three minutes while everyone gaped and exchanged greetings. Wrapping paper and ribbons were recognizable as old friends, saved from year to year along with the ornaments.

If my family members were away due to their various schedules, Pauline was almost always accessible. She had set up an office in our living room to handle the Humphrey-Weidman tours, and a tricycle trip to her desk would usually be rewarded with a sweet cough drop. She could not be disturbed, however, to look at a mere bruise. "Don't show it to me unless it's bleeding" was her quip. She proved to be as good as her word. In the summer of 1939 when Bennington and Mills College exchanged faculties, Pauline was my guardian, sharing a berth with me on the three-day train ride and an apartment at Mills. While crossing the Continental Divide in the middle of the night, I summoned the courage to wake her up to tell her I was bleeding profusely from the nose. She went into action and grabbed the first piece of cloth at hand to stop it. In the morning she discovered that it was her brassiere.

That summer Pauline nursed me through an intestinal illness caused by eating overripe apricots, cleaned me up after I fell into a muddy pond and burst into the faculty dining room, dripping with slime. She took me to the San Francisco World's Fair, and arranged a picnic under the eucalyptus trees for my sixth birthday.

Our New York apartment was often the site of Pauline's costume-making activities. Huge pots of dye would appear in the kitchen along with intensive ironing sessions. Our apartment was also the place where Betty Joiner, Pauline's assistant, who had taken up residence for a time in the back bedroom, crafted the fashion-designer gas masks for the satirical "Air Raid" scene in Charles' *This Passion*. Of course, everyone had to try them on.

Whether for lack of money or forgetfulness, the electric company had not been paid, and the power was suddenly shut off right at the time of the Joe Louis/Max Schmelling boxing match and in the middle of Pauline's costume preparations. Undaunted, Charles and José tapped the radio and extension cord into one of the landlord's hallway outlets and cheered on Joe Louis while Pauline continued her ironing.

When I was five, my governess Marga left to take care of another boy, and with her went several of the rituals to which I had become accustomed. One was the nightly fifteen-or-so minutes I spent with my mother. Part of this time involved doing a moderately painful exercise devised by her and my pediatrician called "curl toes," which involved walking for several minutes with my toes curled under my feet. This exercise was supposed to cure flat feet. Heaven forbid that the son of Doris Humphrey should have flat feet! A misdiagnosis as it turned out. Following "curl toes" and a goodnight kiss, I was taken back to my bedroom where, in Christopher Robin fashion, I said a prayer for every member of my family before turning out the light.

The world that I knew in my early childhood came to an abrupt end in August, 1941. I had spent the summer at Bucks Rock Camp, which was filled with children who had been evacuated during the London blitz. As news spread that their neighborhoods were being destroyed, I began to wonder if I would have a home to come back to in New York! Returning to Tenth Street, I found that the electricity and gas had been shut off and my extended family had gone. José was living in San Francisco. Charles had his own apartment. Pauline had moved to a hotel.

The curtain had come down. I was eight years old.

The scene shifts to the little one-room apartment at Twenty East Thirteenth Street where in 1942 José and Pauline lived after they were married and had moved back from San Francisco. In this tiny space which contained two black beds with yellow spreads, a chair, a dining table, and Pauline's files, José pulled back the rug and created *Chaconne*.

Four months later, José was drafted into the Army. I remember walking down Fifth Avenue with him on one of his first leaves. He was in full uniform, and I was hoping that we would meet an officer so that I could see him salute. Here was a real GI Joe in contrast to my own less glamorous Merchant Marine father who wore only civvies. While José was in the Army, Pauline kept his name alive in the dance world by sending out press releases about his activities. I began to spend my after-school time at the Limóns where I did my homework and helped Pauline with filing. After José was discharged and had started his own company, I helped route the tours with *The Official Guide to the Railways*.

One night at dinner my mother told me that I must never again mention Charles Weidman's name in José's presence. I didn't know why, but could only imagine that there would be an explosion if I did. I never learned what actually happened between José and Charles, but needless to say, I followed my mother's advice. Charles ceased to be a member of my "family." There was only one more brief encounter between us in 1949 at Connecticut College when I was helping backstage at the Weidman Company's performance of *The War Between Men and Women*. I remember that he smelled like the burning brandy on the Cherries Jubilee Pauline served at Thanksgiving and Christmas.

The weekends and summers at the farm were gone, and by the end of the war, when I was fifteen years old, Pauline, José, and I felt confined living in small apartments. We began to yearn for a place in the country.

My mother and father did not share this urge with us. My father was used to living in ships' staterooms and needed little space to be content. My mother, who had grown up in a hotel in Chicago, was satisfied with sleeping on a sofa bed in our living room. The Limóns and I, however, needed space and began to look for it out of New York.

Following up a *New York Times* ad for a barn with twenty-five acres, we took the train to Flemington, New Jersey, on a cold February day in 1948. The realtor drove us to a working dairy barn with piles of manure steaming among the remains of the last snowstorm. It was love at first sight. The only problem was that José did not have the four thousand dollars to buy the barn. The realtor suggested that he talk to the owner, Mrs. Baldwin, who was eighty-six years old. During the course of the conversation, Mrs. Baldwin asked José about his work, and he proceeded to tell her the story of *Day on Earth*. Because she was enchanted by the life-cycle story of the piece and because she took an instant liking to him, Mrs. Baldwin agreed to give José the mortgage he needed.

The barn and its remodeling would occupy the rest of José's life.

On our first night at the barn, we set up army cots in the granary with a cow and calf mooing in another wing. Flies descended on our faces in the morning. Our immediate task was to attack them with all available weapons: spray, swatters, and fly paper. Next in importance was to remove the manure. We created a cooking pit out of stones, grilled our food, and ate under the stars. Mrs. Baldwin called us "gypsies."

That winter we spread our sleeping bags over cots and slept in the unheated loft of the wagon shed. José and I collected stones from stream beds and roadsides to build the stone foundation for the cabin in a former pig pen, which would become our next winter's shelter. We put extra lime in the mortar to keep it from freezing. Meanwhile, our hands were freezing, and we periodically warmed them over an open fire.

The second winter was a little warmer because the cabin had a fireplace where you could easily be broiled if you stood directly in front of it. There was no insulation, and the water in the pails brought from Mrs. Baldwin's house was regularly frozen in the morning. Then fate intervened. A windstorm blew down part of the main barn, and José was able to collect enough money from his insurance claim to begin remodeling. Eventually, it turned into a handsome residence and studio befitting José's large stature.

It was years before we had central heating. Our winter routine revolved around the cold. We would arrive in José's Jeep on Friday night, build the largest fire possible in the fireplace, and fortify ourselves with Martinis or Manhattans while Pauline prepared dinner. These meals were always hearty and delicious, for not only was Pauline business manager, accompanist, costume designer, and adviser, but she was also a wonderful cook. Always protective of José and aware of his proclivity for making hasty commitments, before he answered the phone she would tell him "Whoever it is, the answer is no!"

Soon after my mother died in 1958, my father married another dancer, Joyce Trisler, who was outspoken against José. She claimed that she disliked his "machismo." On his part, José thought that she was an inadequate replacement for Doris Humphrey in our circle. Pauline was confounded by the unsuitability of the match (but she was not entirely uncritical of my father's marriage to my mother either) saying of their union "He never knew what hit him." Nor could I accept Joyce as my stepmother since she was a year younger than I. More than that, I did not like the way that she took over my father. Tall, domineering, and abrasive, she would stroll with her arm looped around his neck as though he were a puppy dog. Martha Hill, who had introduced them and who had hosted their wedding reception, confided to me that although she admired Joyce as a beautiful dancer, she agreed that she was not necessarily someone you would want in your family. My father, however, was always under the spell of whatever woman he was with. Because of the friction between the Limóns and Joyce, he stopped all contact with José and Pauline after the marriage. Joyce had become *persona non grata* in my family. This put a severe strain on my relationship with my father, but my loyalty was clear. I remained devoted to the Limóns whom I had long considered my second parents.

In the last scene at the finished barn José and Pauline are sitting in front of the fireplace in their kitchen/dining room having cocktails at the end of the day. They have both spent the day gardening or, perhaps, José has just returned from a rehearsal in New York. A fragrant pot au feu or burgundy beef simmers on the stove. There is a mood of total contentment that reflects the words of Ecclesiastes immediately following the famous passage that José used for *There Is a Time*: there is nothing better than to be happy, to eat and drink, and to take pleasure in all your toil.

A few weeks before he died, José unexpectedly brought up the subject of Charles Weidman, telling me never to have anything to do with him. What could have been on his mind? That I would turn to Charles once he was gone? Loyalty was paramount in my dance family.

Touchingly, upon learning of José's death, Charles sent a bouquet of roses.

What do I owe to my family? From my mother I inherited practicality, economy, the work ethic, and a critical sense. From Marga I learned discipline and the love of nature, from Charles, I learned to have fun. I experienced the breakup of Humphrey-Weidman as a child of a divorce. Afterward, José and Pauline filled the void as surrogate parents with their unconditional love, the kind that can be passed from one generation to another. From my navigator father and from my own experience in the Navy, I learned to steer a course through shifting currents. Like other children, I wished that my family could have stayed together, but I came to realize that the most satisfying family would be the one that I would have to create for myself.

7

THOMAS SKELTON, LIGHTING DESIGNER

Jennifer Tipton

The trip to Australia was endlessly long; the night seemed to last for days. I was extremely nervous. Tom Skelton had chosen me to be stage manager for the José Limón Company on its trip to the Far East in 1965 and when he left the tour, I was to be in charge of the lighting. In addition to being nervous, I was thrilled. It was my first trip outside the United States and the company was to perform in Australia, Singapore, Malaysia, Thailand, Cambodia, the Philippines, Hong Kong, Taiwan, Korea and Japan. What an adventure! I knew that I was to learn about lighting dance and touring from the "master of light" himself. I could not believe my good fortune.

Tom had already made sure that I spent hours drawing on paper the focus of each light from its position on the stage so that I would not have any insecurity or questions once I had to do it for real. The company carried its own lights, drapery and sound; it had crew chiefs who were responsible for operating the light and sound equipment and for supervising the locally recruited crew in each installation. It was here in Australia that we were to put the production together for the first time and Tom was to establish the way that each dance should look for the rest of the tour. Once he left, it would be my responsibility to see that the dances remained looking the same from one theater to the next. It was here in Australia that Tom began to show me how to make adjustments for unforeseen obstacles, how to get crews to cooperate, how to train my eye to see the need to compensate for various problems, and it was here in Australia that I first began to fall in love with José's beautiful dances as they were revealed by Tom's beautiful light.

Once the performances were completed in Australia, we went on to Asia. A place that I particularly remember now is Seremban, Malaysia. The crew, under Tom's direction, spent a very long day transforming a "high school" type of auditorium into a professional looking theater by hanging black velour drapery around the stage. We even hung black velour borders across the front of the proscenium wall with gaffer's tape. And it didn't fall down! The space looked beautiful. There were many tricks I learned from Tom on that tour. Perhaps the wisest was to learn enough of the local language to be able to say at least "hello", "thank you" and "have a good day" to the locally recruited crew. As we went from place to place I never ceased to be amazed by Tom's quick ear and his ability to pick up useful words. As stage manager and cue caller I proceeded to learn to count in the language of each of the countries we visited.

That trip to Southeast Asia with the Limón Company was very special for me. It was the first time that I had a position with so much responsibility and although I was to travel again with the company, the Asian tour was the only one that allowed me to spend so much time with Tom learning about light and life in the theater. At that moment, in my mind, he knew "everything" and I wanted to learn it. In getting to know his lighting for the Limón repertory as intimately as I did on this tour and later tours in the United States, however, I was able to learn from his light much more than he could ever say in words.

In subsequent years on several occasions I traveled in the U.S. with the Limón company where I was in charge of reproducing Tom's lighting. The economic situation for modern dance companies at the time made it too expensive to travel with drapery or many lights. I was the only non-dancer traveling with the company so I performed the functions of both stage manager and company manager. We carried eight lights and eight stanchions to augment the lighting instruments that we found in the theaters where the company performed, but we carried no black velour drapery.

In the late 1960's, if a company was funded by the New York State Council for the Arts, it had to "repay" the grant by touring to cities in New York State outside of New York City. Local presenters in these cities had little or no experience with the needs of professional dance companies on tour. There was rarely adequate publicity, stage equipment or, for that matter, an appropriate facility for dance. On one Limón tour of upstate New York, several performances were scheduled in spaces where no side masking existed. José in frustration demanded that I find a way to put up wings to hide the dancers when they were offstage. I told him that there was just no way to do that. We had no black velour drapery, no money to rent any and even if we had there was no way to hang it in the Colgate chapel where we were scheduled to perform that night. He demanded that I go to a dormitory and get sheets. I did as I was told and I will never forget the look of *A Choreographic Offering* and *Missa Brevis* in that setting as long as I live. How happy I was that Tom was not there. How I thought back to Seremban and longed for the black velour borders, gaffer's tape, and a crew to hang them!

Thomas Skelton was the lighting designer for the José Limón Dance Company from the early 50's, until José's death in 1972. It was at this

Thomas Skelton. Collection of Heinz Poll.

time that Tom began to define his own ideas about light onstage. It was undoubtedly his love of and devotion to the Limón repertory that led him to discover many of the ideas that remained with him for the rest of his life. By lighting *The Moor's Pavane, The Emperor Jones,* and *The Traitor* he developed his sense of the dramatic: his ideas about light shining from the outside in, from the inside out, and his ideas about no color crosslight. In lighting the dances *Missa Brevis, There is a Time* and *A Choreographic Offering* he refined his ability to make a stage space shimmer with color. During this period he began to develop the idea of having two different, fairly saturated colors together on stage, one from the left and the other from the right, cut through by light with no color in it. This no-color light usually came from the ends of the pipes over the stage. The combination gave his lighting a rich and luscious look that was entirely in tune with the Mexican temperament and aesthetic of José. Tom always had clear backlight (coming from upstage and overhead) making the dancers stand out from the background. This device also made the space sparkle.

Tom was the resident lighting designer for the American Dance Festival (ADF) then at Connecticut College in New London during many of the summers when the Limón company was in residence there. It was an opportunity for him to learn and to teach. Many young dancers and designers had their first taste of the effects of different kinds of light on stage when they studied with him there. It was here that I first met him in a class he taught; it was a class that changed my life. Tom was a remarkable teacher. Formally, he taught at the Yale University School of Drama in the design department from 1976 until 1981, but the truth was that he taught wherever he was and whatever he did. He had a wonderful way of working with young designers, throwing them into new situations but always seeming to know when it would be too much to handle, therefore never pushing too far or too fast. A young person, like myself on the Asian tour, came away from the experience with a sense of accomplishment and the thrill of having done the work well; it was just the thing to encourage a young designer to develop a love for lighting the stage and an abiding belief in his or her own ability to survive and to flourish.

In his position as resident designer at ADF he had an opportunity to see and light all kinds of dance and to work with many of the companies who performed there. At that time performers rarely traveled with their own lighting designers. A performer or company would arrive at Connecticut College in the afternoon before the scheduled evening concert and depend upon Tom to make it look the way it should. Often they left it to him to decide what way that was. I remember an occasion when a solo performer left the stage during a rehearsal, came into the house to check the light and said to Tom, "Oh it looks so flat. You better turn on more front light." Tom turned on more **side** light and the performer went back to the stage happy with the way it looked. From this I learned an invaluable lesson. Analyze the problem; don't accept someone else's solution.

Tom was a wizard at grasping the essence of the style of movement and working quickly to light it in such a way that would allow the audience to grasp it as well. I was often in awe of the great variety of looks that Tom produced on stage, always appropriate to the dance, the company and the place.

Tom lit many dancers and companies in addition to the Limón company. He was very drawn to ethnic dance which led him to extensive travel. His interest and ability brought him to the attention of the impresario Sol Hurok who asked him to supervise the lighting for many companies from all over the world that toured the States. Tom lit the work of companies from Bali, Taiwan, Korea and Mexico, among many others. He made a trip to the Ivory Coast where he was invited to see many masked dances, some for men's eyes only. He was there to help develop a company that never materialized, but the effect of the dance that he saw in Africa was profound both on his life and on his art. During this time he began a relationship with the Ballet Hispanico de Mexico that was to last for a number of years. It was for this company perhaps more than any other where his sense of color was most fully explored and developed.

Tom lit ballet and modern dance equally well. The Robert Joffrey Company and the Paul Taylor Company boasted Skelton lighting from their very beginnings. The experience that he gained from lighting these two companies and the Limón company, three quite diverse forms of dance, as well as the many dancers and other small companies that he lit from time to time, gave him a perspective that was beyond compare. It was also with these three companies that he began to learn the demands of touring a repertory company. His lighting was created with the thought that it should be done quickly and easily in each new theater, and that the repertory should have the same look in every theater in which it would be performed. He was opposed aesthetically to the idea that there be a New York version and a touring version. His knowledge of ballet, modern dance and ethnic dance made him a very accomplished and desirable lighting designer for dance of all kinds and he was often asked to light evenings of dance, programs that had a mixture of dance styles, choreographed by several people. From these events he further developed his sense of how a program should be arranged, how the light for one dance went with that of another, and how a dance could be made more visible, more accessible the dances placed before and after it.

Arguably, Tom Skeleton became THE lighting designer for dance in New York City and perhaps the world in the 60's and 70's, but his experience and his intellectual acumen made him much more than just a lighting designer. He had learned about theater space, about every aspect of mounting dance productions and of making them happen on stage, about good programming and many other things. He spent his last years devoted to the Ohio Ballet as lighting designer, with added responsibilities of consulting director and administrator, with his dear friend and companion, Heinz Poll.

But dance was not his only love. Tom lit plays, musicals and opera with the same passion and insight. One of the endearing qualities about him and his work was the profound personal commitment he made to the people that he designed for and consequently to their aesthetic. With Tom it was never just a job; there was always a deep love of light and how it graced the stage and the people. His was a design of concepts and ideas, not just pretty looks. He was always aware of how the light shaped the space and how the space affected the light. With that kind of eye, it is only natural that he would be a wonderful space maker – set designer – and indeed he designed scenery on several occasions, notably for the Pennsylvania Ballet's production of *The Sleeping Beauty*.

As successful lighting designers are prone to do, Tom very early in his life became busy with overlapping jobs and obligations. He developed a shorthand for planning and doing light plots while traveling on air planes. He would often meet an assistant at a distant airport for a planning meeting, he on the way to one city and the assistant passing through the same airport by coincidence, or more likely by plan. They would work together for a time before each had to catch a plane to the next destination. Despite his ability to work "on the fly", he was committed to the drafting board as a tool. By drafting the plan and many sections of the theater space, he was able to tell what the focus should be and was able to go into a theater unknown by him with confidence that the lights could be made to work. Confidence, however, is a strange word to use when describing Tom. His nervous energy and deep passion for the work at hand made him extremely tense about any new production, new venue or new situation. His lighting always seemed to reveal his inner state, a complex mixture of color and texture that never settled in one place but was always alive. Tom's lighting always conveyed an emotion that was in harmony with the work he was lighting. This heightened sense of feeling that was in Tom's lighting was perfectly in tune with the Limón repertory. This was perhaps because the seeds were planted in the early years of their collaborations when their mutual respect and trust were established.

Tom Skelton was an old fashioned romantic, both as a person and as a lighting designer. He came from Maine and grew up in New England, far from José Limón's Mexico both geographically and temperamentally, but there was some inner spirit and passion that the two men had shared in the way they had lived and the way they had made theater together. It was my great honor to have worked with them both.

8

LUCAS HOVING AND JOSÉ LIMÓN: RADICAL DANCERS

Ann Murphy

Sixty years ago American modern dance was a fervent kingdom of women – priestesses, goddesses, sirens and liberators. Men were few in number, and when they did appear, they were often as one-dimensionally heroic as the women were heroically complex.

Then came José Limón and Lucas Hoving. José's taut choreography found its perfect vehicle in the juxtaposition of his form against Lucas', and together the two men dancing created a spiritual rhythm similar to the play of convex and concave in the vault of a Baroque church. But the collaboration went further than the aesthetic. During ten years of intense partnership, and fourteen years of association, these two men expanded the terrain of modern dance by giving unprecedented richness not only to male expression but to men in relationship to one another. They ignored the roles men had so often played in dance as symbols of virility or handsome scenery, and created instead a fictive world of flawed psychological men, passionately and often tragically engaged in the complex drama of living. And by offering a truer glimpse of the dynamic between men, the relations within and across the sexes came clearer. Thickets of power, emotion and desire that trap their subjects – this was how José saw social relations and it was through them rather than polemic that José asked questions about right and wrong, good and evil.

Both Lucas and José were born as modernism and the modern era took form, and they came of age as the latent conflicts between the 19th and 20th centuries erupted. José was born in the Mexican province of Sinaloa on January 12, 1908, the same year Henry Ford designed the Model T and two years before the start of the Mexican Revolution. Lucas was born on September 5, 1912 in the northern medieval Dutch city of Groningen, bordering the German province of Lower Saxony. In 1910 Picasso painted his cubist "Nude Woman." In 1913 Igor Stravinsky wrote "Rite of Spring," which caused a riot at the Paris Opera House. A year later World War I broke out.

The 1920's have mythic appeal now. It was a sizzling decade fueled by radical experimentation and the rise of the new, with Paris and Berlin the

capitals. But it was also beset by crumbling ancient orders, hunger, decadence, joblessness and, ultimately, violent extremism. By the 1930's chaos
and despair were tightening their grip. It is hard to conceive today, in
spite of political attacks on the arts in the U. S. Congress, but Lucas along
with the other members of the dance company of Florrie Rodrigo, a
Dutch Communist and a Jew, fled Holland around 1935 under increasingly dire threat from the Dutch fascists. Rodrigo's dance themes ranged
from workers' oppression to the rise of concentration camps, and while
the fascists' disruptive tactics didn't stop them, police censorship did.

Florencio Limón, José's father, was a poor, proud musician of Spanish
and French extraction who led traveling military bands in his job as
director of the State Music Academy of Sonora. José's mother, Traslaviña,
was a mix of Spanish and Indian, and was 16 when she married the
35-year-old widower with two children. Within the year she bore José,
the first of her own brood. In 1910 revolution sprang up across Mexico
and chaos flared like brush fire as the peasantry heeded Emilio Zapata's
battle cry "Bread and land!" José's family got caught in the crossfire.

In 1913 fighting erupted in their town, and the Limón house was in the
battle zone of the Zapatistas and the federales. Artillery fire flew, a bullet
catching his uncle in the head. For days, according to Charles Humphrey
Woodford, Doris Humphrey's son, the rest of the family hid in their cel-
lar, where his mother and infant sister lay ill, until the siege ended and
they could collect themselves and flee north toward the border.

Destitute, his father traveled to Arizona in hopes of finding work, and
there took a job as conductor of a Southern Pacific Railroad band and
orchestra. In 1915, the family followed. Eventually they pushed west to
Los Angeles where Florencio supported the family as a private cello and
clarinet teacher and as a part-time band leader. In José's eyes it was a
poor but cultured family.

Lucas was the descendent of farmers and the petit bourgeoisie. His
sullen, frustrated father was a butcher, whose shop sat at the front of
their boarding house in the center of the city and was stocked by his
farm. His mother, who developed rheumatoid arthritis after Lucas was
born, was an invalid for most of his childhood and daily stationed herself in a chair in the kitchen where she could run the household, oversee-
ing the odd characters and suppressing illicit dalliances. She relied on
Lucas from the time he was very young for assistance dressing, getting
out of bed, and struggling to the kitchen.

Like Doris Humphrey, whose parents ran a hotel, and Pina Bausch,
whose parents owned and operated a cafe, Lucas was exposed to a far
larger and more sophisticated world than his family alone could ever
have provided. Among the boarders at the Hovingas were university
students and a pianist for the local dance hall who kept an upright in his

room. By the age of three Lucas was plucking out melodies from the piano keys. He was a musical prodigy, the pianist said, and at thirteen, after years of trading steaks and chops from his father's shop for music lessons, Lucas found himself as an accompanist in the dance world. He played first for the Eclecta Club of rhythmical gymnastics, then for Wigman-trained dancer Neel Kuiper, who transformed the club into a modern dance school.

In 1926 José, whose precocious artistic talent led him on a path as a painter, fled the frustrations of UCLA, Los Angeles, his young mother's death and the gaggle of younger children in the family. He awkwardly made his way East and arrived in New York looking for the world.

As the years progressed, poverty deepened across the western world, and opportunities for artists in Europe evaporated. Lucas left the continent altogether in 1938, with a scholarship in hand to the Folkwang Schule in exile at Dartington Hall in England. Kurt Jooss, school director Sigurd Leeder, and the members of the Ballets Jooss had eluded a Nazi dragnet in Essen four years earlier and made their way to safety outside London. Rudolf von Laban sought refuge there as well. The heart of German modern dance had moved to England.

In the U.S., while the threat of fascism didn't exist, banks closed, farms failed, poverty struck from coast to coast. Franklin Roosevelt buoyed the U.S. with social welfare programs. Collective, family-like structures sprang up in theater and dance, ranging from Lee Strasberg's Group Theatre to the New Dance Group, spurred by a combination of poverty and idealism. Federal financing never did make as direct an impact on the dance world as it did in theater with the Federal Theatre Project (employing 10,000 people at its peak), but the spirit of community and democracy of the day did. José experienced it intimately in the work and workshops as well as in the collective household Doris Humphrey created. Lucas knew it from the household he had shared with Rodrigo and fellow dancers in Amsterdam and Brussels, and felt it when he arrived in New York with the Jooss company. It was this spirit that José and Lucas deeply shared.

Something else linked them as well. Long before they met, Lucas and José each had an epiphany that shaped their futures. At different moments on separate continents, they went to the theater and saw the renowned German dancer Harald Kreutzberg perform. Master actor, wizard of ritualized expression, protégé of theater director Max Reinhardt and dancer Mary Wigman, and part of the famed couple of Kreutzberg and Yvonne Georgi, Kreutzberg redefined dance for each of them. "What I saw simply and irrevocably changed my life," José wrote in Selma Jeanne Cohen's *The Modern Dance*. "I saw dance as a vision of ineffable power. A man could, with dignity and towering majesty, dance."

Kreutzberg was unlike other male dancers of the period. His primitive style with its thrusting, angular shapes and jagged rhythms, its mesmerizing use of repetitions, its exquisite delicacy and potent volume had been pioneered by Wigman under Rudolph von Laban's tutelage. But no man in American modern dance had translated such material into his own world before or adopted such pansexual expression. Kreutzberg could play a witch one moment, the devil the next, and then a powerful temptress who also dances the role of her victim, a country farmer. José, watching Kreutzberg, became seized that night by the conviction that he had to be a dancer. "Kreuzberg," he wrote, "had given me the illumination to see the road. But he was German; his visions were Gothic. They became him; but I was by origin a Mexican, reared in the United States. I must find the dance to say what I had to say about what I was."

Lucas was riveted by Kreutzberg's androgyny. Kreutzberg seemed, he said, "to be feminine one moment and masculine the next. You didn't know what he was." Ironically, Lucas was plucked from obscurity in 1937 by Kreutzberg's former partner, Yvonne Georgi, who, after seeing Lucas dance, enlisted the 25-year-old Dutchman to take Kreutzberg's place.

* * *

The picture José and Lucas made as a pair is now one of the easiest details for people to recall of the two men's ten years together. José had a high, fine bone structure that looked windswept and regal. He was smoke-dark like his Yaqui ancestors, and his physical body emitted a power and weight that lent him a regal earthiness fit for an Indian leader.

Lucas was thin, sharp-faced, blond and angular. His joints protruded when he moved and in his arching and twisting body there was lyricism and line to equal José's muscular drama. As a pair, they not only embodied physical and temperamental opposites, they manifested the poles of American society – the dark-skinned exotic indigenous man and the fair European who, through a kind of cultural primogeniture, would always be welcome. Bill T. Jones and Arnie Zane were, in many respects, a latter-day version of Limón and Hoving.

These two men, both just over six feet tall, were not radicals in the manner of a Rosa Luxemburg, who lived and died for social revolution, or Clifford Odets, who wrote socialist plays. Nor were they dancer-activists as were Anna Sokolow or Helen Tamiris. They joined no political parties, and never devoted time to pamphleteering or espousing doctrines of social justice. They were closer in type to the pioneer generation of Humphrey and Graham who came just before them. Critic and historian Marcia Siegel, in her biography of Doris Humphrey, *Days on Earth*, says of these earliest modern dancers that they "wanted to speak

Lucas Hoving and José Limón in *The Emperor Jones*.
Photo by Bogdan Krasicki. Limón Archives.

for their times and their people, but they were essentially humanists and idealists." What distinguished José and Lucas from them was that the young dancers were immigrants driven from politically volatile worlds where the drama of politics, which was not abstract but pointedly human, saturated every aspect of life and was inseparable from the humanism they held dear.

Lucas from a young age felt that fate directed his life. He let it determine the course of events in New York in 1946 after the war and his life-altering years in the Royal Dutch Army. "I'd never heard of José before I met him," Hoving said. "We had both been in the army and were hiding in the back of Nanette Charisse's Vaganova class trying to get in shape again after the war. Neither of us was a ballet dancer, and because of the army we hadn't worked for so long. You know how in ballet class you see yourself in the mirror? There weren't many men there then, and the contrast between the two of us was really striking. He was weighty and heavy; I was much lighter and lyrical. We were different in every respect. That got us together."

Lucas soon went to see José in a performance at the Humphrey-Weidman studio at West 16th St. "I remember how impressive José was," Lucas said. "He had such presence, strength and real authority. He was in a trio with two women [possibly Beatrice Seckler and Dorothy Bird] and I decided I wanted to dance with José after that. I thought his presence was very beautiful and strong."

Sometime in the following months, José went to see Lucas perform. "A Jooss dancer staged a piece for one of the young choreographers' workshops in which I had a wonderful role," Lucas explained. José was impressed, and Lucas let him know that if the chance came, he wanted to dance with him.

In 1947 José formalized his break from the Humphrey-Weidman family – it had started unraveling before the war when his romantic relationship to Charles Weidman ended – by launching the José Limón Dance Company. Then he reconstituted his connection to Humphrey by naming her artistic director and advisor to the new troupe. The next year, at a moment when Lucas seemed flooded with invitations from such choreographers as Martha Graham and Valerie Bettis, which often included a place for his wife Vinnie (Lavina Nielsen), José asked Lucas to join the fledgling company.

Lucas had danced under the direction of women for most of his career – Valerie Bettis, Catherine Littlefield, Agnes DeMille as well as Graham and Rodrigo – and under Jooss he functioned something like a new member of a corps de ballet whose job was to learn the repertory and fit into the dances as seamlessly as possible. Had he got to join in making dances with Jooss, Lucas might not have felt the same need to dance with José. But Jooss had hired Lucas to learn the parts of a German dancer who rushed home when war broke out, and a mere week after Lucas began, the company launched its tours through the British Isles and South America. Jooss, meanwhile, was interned in England as a citizen of an enemy country. The company tour went on without him. The travel lasted nearly two years until finally, broke and marooned in the U.S. because of the war, the troupe was forced to disband.

Lucas felt that he would like to work with a man again and that this time, with a new, burgeoning company, he would have more chance for artistic freedom and collaboration. When Lucas and José finally began work together they sniffed each other out like two species of cat. "I'd sit and look at him dance," Lucas said, "then he'd look at me and how I moved. We walked around each other, cased each other."

"He could be very warm and open on stage, but his strong side was the first thing I saw in his dancing. In Jooss everything you danced was always central or peripheral to the body, central movement being from the front of the body, peripheral movement being from the periphery. José didn't have that separation at all."

With José, not only was the work new but process was everything. "We dragged the pieces, which were mostly dramatic, out from nowhere," Lucas explained. "José didn't work on the character of a role very much. He'd say: 'I see such and such.' I'd get it right away in the body, then he'd start the movement, and I'd pick it up. Gradually I got the feeling of what the character was and how it should move. Then I would say 'Look, this is what I get.' I'd try something and he'd say 'That's right, that's right!' We had a very good relationship creatively," Lucas explained. "José spoke beautifully, and very baroquely…but he couldn't speak about the things that came from deep down. He was a primitive." He was also the authority.

"He knew more or less what he wanted – he gave you about 80% of the movement, the rest you could add. I think he always had the music before he started. It was a beautiful way of working, because he'd give you all the space you needed to stay your own person, and the roles he had for me were very different. He was always generous in praising the results."

As José's advisor and director, Doris opposed José's choice – Lucas, she said, wasn't right for the kind of movement she and José choreographed. Nor did she like Betty Jones, Lucas recalled, presumably because Betty came from Broadway, where art house dance was sacrificed to commercial values. On both counts, José ignored Doris' advice.

In Lucas' accounts of his years with the company, Doris comes across as a sort of shadow figure, like an oppressive mother hovering in the wings, and there is little sense of her as the spiritual beacon José deeply relied on. Lucas remains ambivalent about the pioneer choreographer and "foster mother" of José, as Limón described her, who shepherded the young choreographer's talents and edited his compositions, and who was already in a great deal of pain, suffering from the severe arthritis that plagued the final period of her life. Whether Lucas was reacting to echoes of his own arthritic mother, her cool personality, Doris' analytical style, or her influence over José is unclear. He liked few of her dances, and forty years later he is still irked by the control Doris and Pauline Lawrence, Doris' accompanist, costumer, passionate friend and ultimately, José's wife, had over José. He recounts how, after a performance and before a party, the two women took a look at José and said "You can't possibly wear that shirt. Get another." And, dutifully, to Lucas' shock, José obeyed.

Yet even before Lucas' wife Vinnie joined the company with the 1952 dance *There is a Time*, Lucas, Vinnie and Doris developed a daily rhythm together that included Doris in their suppertime retreat to their apartment on 55th St. to eat and rest with them between afternoon (3–6 pm) and evening (8–11 pm) rehearsals at the City Center studio on 56th St. "We lived very close to the studio and Vinnie was always extremely generous saying 'Doris, come home, Doris, come rest, I'll cook a meal.' So during rehearsal periods we saw a lot of Doris. We became very good friends."

"But Doris didn't really teach us," he explains, " – she was rehearsal director – and I never went to take class at the Humphrey-Weidman studio. I didn't think it was all that interesting. Charles Weidman was funny and could do comic dance, and Doris did several pieces for the Limón Company that were all right, if you wanted to dance clearly and exactly. But until *Ruins and Visions* I never danced anything by Doris that I enjoyed. José brought a whole new life to Humphrey-Weidman, you see. It came from his Mexican soul."

What his Mexican soul brought, in part, was a celebration of male beauty. But even more important, José centralized the strengths and flaws of men. Not that others hadn't tried. Ted Shawn and Charles Weidman made forays into the arena of male-centered dance, Weidman, for example, creating *Ringside* in 1932 as a study for men of boxers' movements, and Ted Shawn, endorsing the machismo of dance through such all-male spectacle as *Kinetic Molpai*. But much of this sort of fare was either decorative or sentimentally reduced men to tantalizing objects of brawn, often suggestively uncovered. José and Lucas, by contrast, found an ambiguity and passion together which translated into potent male-male duets that were neither the dances strictly of lovers or of buddies (José and Lucas were both bisexual, married men), but something in between, something polymorphous and androgynous. While often abiding by traditional

Lucas Hoving and José Limón in rehearsal of *The Traitor*. Photo by Matthew Wysocki. The Louis Horst Collection of The Dance Collection, New York Public Library.

masculine content of hero and anti-hero in the narrative structure of the dances, José and Lucas explored the under-lying eroticism in the bonds of hate and love, fealty and betrayal. As a result, their passionate counterpoint on stage often shared some of the same charismatic intensity of heterosexual duets at the heart of classical ballet.

One of the ways José fashioned such suggestive theater was by reaching deeply into an arena of moral drama and existential pathos. This led to dances that on the group level were usually relational and communal but which structurally, and on the plane of the individual, often formed a series of taut pairings, triangulations and cross pairings. Nowhere is this more evident than in the elegant cat's cradle, *The Moor's Pavane*, which, in its kinesthetic and psychological architecture, is a stately map of human frailty worthy of Shakespeare's original. José implicitly used these geometries to explore the ambiguity of desire and its ethical consequences. Arguably the material surrounded him – from the passionate friendships of Doris and his wife Pauline and him and Lucas, to the beneficial symbiosis that he and Doris shared.

On the level of stylistic development, he brought German *Ausdruckstanz* (the term used to describe German expressive dance of that period) back from the exotica and atavism of Kreutzberg into more traditional dramatic form. Such narratives as the Judas tale in *The Traitor* and the tragedy of Othello in *The Moor's Pavane* anchored the drama of his relationship to Lucas (the Christ figure in the former, and the diabolical Iago in the latter), in the linear sweep of tragedy. At the same time he maintained the symbolic heft of *Ausdruckstanz* by sculpting movement that often was as magnetic, compressed and sere as Mary Wigman's or flamenco.

The first dance they collaborated on was *La Malinche*, the drama of Cortez' conquest of Mexico and the Indian princess, Malintzin, who, seduced by the conqueror, betrays her people then returns as La Malinche after her death to lead the Indians in revolution. Lucas took his first evil Limón role as the Conquistador. Pauline Koner danced the role of the wild Malinche, and José danced El Indio, the Indian everyman.

As Lucas notes in the video documentary, *Touching the Souls* by Tony Kramer, he didn't really dance with José in *La Malinche* but with Pauline Koner, as Malintzin, through whom Lucas as the Conquistador conquers El Indio, the figure of tragic Mexico. Lucas did, however, get his first taste of Limón's theater and the power and possibility for betrayal in the triangles José devised. "I preferred such dramatic pieces," Lucas explained. "I'm by nature an actor and liked to be a character, not just a dancer."

Triangles multiplied and the sculpted heat between the characters boiled six months later when José unveiled *The Moor's Pavane* at Connecticut College. Lucas and José now met face to face, Lucas as the malevolent Iago, José the tragically credulous Othello.

As *Pavane* opens, decorum rules the two men and two women in their Renaissance attire, and the stately tone never flags, even as treachery brews. In fact the constrained pomp of Purcell's *On the Death of a Princess*, the echoes of highly formal Baroque dance, and the constant presence on stage of all four dancers compress the story until it becomes ritual and takes on aspects of a Kabuki dance of death.

The relation to Japanese theater was more than superficial, according to Lucas. "I only found it out much later after seeing the opera *Otello* that José played his role like an opera singer or a Noh actor," he explained, "whereas Koner and I would maybe play using Stanislavsky's method acting. José would face me and make a face – try to break me up – I couldn't believe it! Then he'd turn front and there was that composed face again. Or he'd look cross-eyed at me, stick his tongue out at times. Night after night on tour you think 'Do I have to do this again?' He could do *that*."

In the archival film with the original cast of José, Lucas, Betty Jones as Desdemona and Pauline Koner as Emilia, the four dancers begin in a circle holding hands, asserting their shared community. Together, they raise their arms above their shoulders, letting their eyes lift toward heaven, as if to acknowledge the enormous forces that will shape everything to come. From this act of obeisance, the men break the circle. Like matadors, they execute a wary, almost predatory rond de jambe to the back, echoed instantly but decorously by the women. José and Lucas then rise into attitude en arrière and clasp their hands together above their heads in a gesture worthy of Samurai warriors. This is followed by a deep lunge into second position on the diagonal.

With these few spare actions, José establishes the dramatic hierarchy of relations: the group, then the pair of men, then the women together, and finally the two couples: Othello and Desdemona, Iago and Emilia.

Throughout *Pavane*, Lucas and José perform with the ineluctability of natural forces. Lucas wraps his lower leg around José with possessiveness not simply because he wants to whisper treachery in José's ear, but because he seeks to own his soul.

A second hierarchy in the dance exists that provides important counter-tension to the dominant structure and, like a secondary voice in a motet or theme in a drama, it echoes and varies the main theme of jealousy and deadly ambition. Here, Emilia rules as wickedly as Iago, consumed by her own indecent jealousies. Although she begins as a pawn of her indifferent husband, she ultimately controls and lustily taunts him with the handkerchief which she has stolen for him. Using it as false evidence of Desdemona's fictive sexual betrayal, Iago in turn manipulates Othello's jealous outrage, and the dance spirals to a close as Othello murders Desdemona then falls in suicide on her prostrate body. In the Limón version of the Shakespeare story, Emilia, as danced by Pauline Koner, is Iago's lesser twin.

The betrayal of Jesus by Judas Iscariot is the subject of *The Traitor* (1954) though its impetus, according to José in his essay "An American Accent", was the execution of the Rosenbergs, charged with being national traitors. Judas, the beloved disciple who adored Jesus more than the other disciples, is, like Iago, impelled by immoderate and ambiguous passions merging love and hate, which cause him to betray Jesus to the Roman military.

As the dance opens, José dancing the role of Judas enters from upstage, darting backwards as he gesticulates tightly in front of his chest. The mood is compulsive, unconscious, deceitful and guilt-ridden. He swipes his left hand across his neck. He executes a loose emboité then soutenus, his wrists meeting behind his back like a prisoner's. He again turns, now in the opposite direction. The space design curls in on itself and his phrases begin to accumulate like repeated licks of a whip.

Lucas in the role of Jesus enters later on the same diagonal *facing* the audience and performing an echo of Judas' angular swiping at his neck, except that Lucas' movement sweeps frontally away from his body and into space rather than neurotically across his torso. It becomes the gesture of benediction rather than anxiety and doom, and this calm generosity of the limbs, which move out into the periphery from the base line of the body, are the antiphon to José's movements, which are forever coiling tortuously in on the body's axis.

The Traitor finds this very mysterious balance between the men, one exalted, one damned, who love one another into death. It is almost as though Othello and Iago had been merged as one character, Judas, and Desdemona were transformed into the exalted innocent, Christ, who, rather than the passive feminine, is the transcendent divine.

Judas is propelled by confusion, unconscious drives and thwarted desire; Jesus is weighed down with his heroic but lonely sorrow. Their final tragic encounter, Jesus standing heroically still, Judas winding the shroud around him, is one of the sparest, most poignant moments in the Limón repertory and captures the searing paradox at the heart of Limón's view of men and tragedy: the victim and the victimizer are as linked as proton and electron. The group of men who surround them throughout this all-male dance are meanwhile a kind of Greek chorus whose character is constantly derived from the action of the protagonists. At the opening of the dance they are disciples who mirror Judas, while at other times they embody brutal Roman soldiers who gamble away lives. Always they exist to orchestrate the action between the alter egos.

Like Joseph Conrad's Marlow who understands that a conqueror's victory "…is just an accident arising from the weakness of others," José grasped that authority, love and duty are often propped up by greedy ambition, lust, guilt and envy. Through his partnership with Lucas, his dances again and again pierced the decorous surface of social links, political structures and psychological relationships, and for the first time in American modern dance history, men mirrored the ambiguous reality of men's lives and the whole of American modern dance grew richer.

9

LIMÓN IN MEXICO; MEXICO IN LIMÓN

Ann Vachon

Over the last five years I have been interviewing dancers who worked with José Limón in both the United States and Mexico, and I have come to understand him in unexpected new ways. Increasingly, I see him as a man caught between cultures, for whom that very conflict made an essential contribution to his artistry. I became Limón's student in 1956, and worked in his company until several years after his death in 1972, without ever distinctly perceiving him as Mexican. Of course I knew he had been born in Mexico, that English was not his first language, and that he had the high cheekbones and dark eyes of a Native American. But since José never spoke of his family or his childhood, I thought of the Mexican part as almost a novelty. America, after all, was a land made of immigrants, and in those days we were operating on the "melting pot" premise. I knew Limón as a cultural ambassador, sent around the world by the United States government, to represent what we thought of as an "indigenous" art form, American Modern Dance. José paid homage to his dance ancestors Isadora Duncan and Doris Humphrey. He was a private person, and didn't talk about his past. In interviews during the last year, people who had known him even better than I, Lucas Hoving, Betty Jones, Pauline Koner and Danny Lewis all said the same thing; he never spoke of his childhood.

I did know that the company had been lavishly received by the Mexican public in the early fifties, and I experienced this myself in 1960, when, as a member of the company, we ended a State Department tour of South and Central America in Mexico City, and performed to cheering audiences in the imposing Palacio de Belles Artes. José very definitely played the host on that visit, inviting the entire company to a sumptuously catered meal, and giving each of us a small engraved silver ashtray as a souvenir of Mexico. We learned that he had previously been invited to remain in Mexico, and had already created several new works there.

Towards the end of his life José began to write about himself, in an unfinished autobiography, and other manuscripts. The autobiography begins with his symbolic birth in 1929, at the Humphrey Weidman studio in New York City, and at 281 handwritten pages, ends with his account of choreographing *Chaconne* in 1942. Although these passages were written when he was in his sixties, they are particularly vivid with childhood memories. Reading this material helped me resolve some of the mysteries I sensed about him, and gave me a deeper understanding of his artistry. Rather than serve as an interpreter in this article, I will include some of the passages I found most revealing about his relationship to his Mexican heritage.

On January 12, 1908, in Culiacán, capital of the state of Sinaloa, Mexico, *"José Limón was delivered, ... kicking like a roped steer."*[1] His father *"a musician, pedagogue, conductor, the director of the State Academy of Music"* and *"a tall rather handsome, distinguished man, a widower of French and Spanish descent."*[2]

> "My first memory of all is of sitting naked in a tub or basin of water in a charming spot. This is most likely the patio of our house in Culiacan where I was born. I was splashing water on myself and my surroundings and on a laughing young woman, my mother. It was golden in the sunlight, and green and cool in the shade. There were beautiful odors. I adored my mother, and she was very happy. I had a toy guitar."[3]
>
> He wrote that his mother "a girl of sixteen, came of a good bourgeois family...." "The Traslaviña's had, like most Mexicans, a dash of Indian blood, which was not too apparent, and which they did their best to forget. It was not considered quite nice, in those times, in respectable provincial society, to be tainted with the blood of the wild tribes of the mountains or deserts, or the peons enslaved in the gigantic "hacienda," or "los plebes," the degraded and poverty-stricken rabble in the cities."[4]

This class consciousness, and a budding ambivalence about it that apparently existed within his own family, reflected challenges that were occurring all around him, in the very ambiance of a country embarking on a class revolution. When José was five years old that conflict encroached on the bliss of his childhood.

> "It happened in the dining room of our house. It was early morning and the family... was at breakfast. Gunfire interrupted the meal. At first it was thought to be the sound of firecrackers. In Mexico the saints like their festivals to be full of music, processions and fireworks. We were disabused when bullets began to shatter the windowpanes and whistle into the room. Pandemonium. My father shouted a command. Everyone hit the floor, except my gallant young uncle. He had to see what was going on and looked out the window.... He fell backward into the room, and a pool of blood grew around him.... My father crawled to the bedrooms, dragged mattresses and quilts which he threw over us. It seems our house was located on a rising slope of a hill between the attacking revolutionary forces and their objective at the summit, a fort held by the Federals, and bullets continued to whistle through the house. At three o'clock there was a truce and the Red Cross picked up my moribund half dead uncle and took him to a hospital where he subsequently died.... I remember being awakened periodically during the night by the sound of machine guns and artillery.... "[5]

The family moved north, to Cananea, where his father became director of the "Academia de Musica" for the state of Sonoma, and conducted public band concerts as well as the orchestra at the local theater. José remembers being captivated by dance that early.

> "There were concerts, dramas, 'zarzuelas,' and the miraculous 'cinematógrafo.' There were variety music hall nights, and on these I remember glittering Spanish dancers, with sumptuos black coiffures, topped elegantly by incredibly high combs, with crimson roses nestling in them, costumed in sequined iridescence. The electrifying pound of castanets, the magnetic intricacy of the steps and figurations, the verve of the 'taconeado', the flurries and cascades of ruffled petticoats, all these moved me to a pitch of excitement which I could neither understand nor explain."[6]

José wrote of seeing Tango dancers, the Can-can and Cakewalk, and he described a human butterfly that reminds one of descriptions of Loie Fuller. An even stronger impression was left on him by the bullfight, which he called "dance – dance at its most proud, formal and elegant, although it was given another designation."

> "It was another facet of the Iberian nature, and as such fascinating, and to be regarded with the curious ambivalence with which a Mexican regards things Spanish. Spain means the conqueror Cortez, the destroyer and despoiler of ancient native cultures, a man wanton, cruel and insatiable. Spain represents three centuries of subjection, of the enslavement and oppression of indigenous populations, of merciless and unscrupulous maltreatment and exploitation. Spain is also the mother country. She gave us 'nuestro Señor Jesu-Cristo' and his crucifix, and his 'Santa Madre, nuestra Señora la santisima Virgen Maria.'
> ... Costumed in great splendor, in breath-taking colors, the bull fighters evoke an age that knew how to enhance the appearance of a man. A man bent on an undertaking gallant, heroic and dangerous. A being consecrated and set apart. A man to perform an ancient ritual drama that would cleanse and purge us, the spectators. A symbol, with symbolic powers and graces and prerogatives ... I did not know, as I watched spellbound and terrified, that I was watching an art whose gesture and movement would influence me profoundly when I in turn became a dancer. I would, in composing dances, look back to this facet of my gestatory period for guidance and inspiration."[7]

Limón wrote eloquently about the inherent ambivalence that was a constant within his Mexican heritage. Later there were other powerful influences on him, but these early memories found their way into his choreography and dancing.

The family moved from place to place in northern Mexico, to Hermosilla, Nogales, where his father worked as an army band leader for various Revolutionary Generals. Then, when José was seven years old they crossed the border to live in the United States.

"At seven years of age I learned what I was to be for the rest of my life, a translator and conciliator. It was to be my task to translate, perpetually, within myself,
the tongue of Castile to that of the Anglo Saxons, to reconcile many disparate and
contradictory cultural habits, ways of living and resolving hostilities, within and
around me. This began even before we crossed the northern frontier, that
formidable and awesome barrier, which, like all boundaries, represents a division
that separates and isolates physically and spiritually. Beyond this line to the
north was the 'Norte Americano,' the 'Yanqui,' the 'Gringo.' He was powerful.
He spoke 'Ingles,' which was a language totally incomprehensible to those who
spoke 'the lingua castellana' or 'español' … He was likely to intervene at any
moment in the Mexican revolution. 'La Intervencion' hung over our heads like
the Damoclean sword. Fear. Dread. To a seven year old these two are palpable,
sickening realities."[8]

He had become an immigrant. His early struggles with the English
language left him with a lifelong determination. After being ridiculed by
his classmates in an early attempt at reading English aloud, he "resolved
a number of things. One was that I would learn this impossible language, whose capricious and illogical pronunciation hadn't the remotest
relation to the way it was written, better than any of those who had
jeered at me."[9] It is evident that indeed he did. I remember his vocabulary
as being prodigious, even if it occasionally took some reflection to find
the precise word. But when he found it, it's appropriateness stunned.

The translating that Limón referred to was not only linguistic. There
were other aspects of the new culture which he had to reconcile. Who,
for example, would be his male role model?

"El Señor don Florencio Limón, the man I little knew and less understood, my
father, my enemy, and a figure of fear, awe, contempt, hatred, and ultimately and
too late, reverence and love, first posed these questions during the first two
decades of my being. Not in so many words, perhaps. Not explicitly. No. He did
it quite simply by example. By the way he lived his daily life. By his behavior in
big and small things. By his language, his voice and intonation, his manner. His
style. Also all his dignity. In Mexico he had been somebody, a man of education
and accomplishment and status. Across the border in Arizona he became one of
many refugees from the chaos to the south."[10]

His father also became the enemy.

"By now I knew that my mother was slowly dying, with one pregnancy, one
child after another, year after year, that the man who was slowly but surely
killing her was my father. I worshipped her. To me she was beautiful and kind
and tender and always loving and understanding. She did not deserve to be
killed like this. Very suddenly I was 18 years old, tall, as tall as my father, dark,
like my mother, and not fair like my father. And the unthinkable happened, and
outside in the hospital corridor I, who had spent the final hours at my mother's
death bed and heard the death rattle become the final incredible long drawn out
sibilance, and had taken the gold wedding band and irrationally slipped it on my
finger, after all these things seen and felt and done in the cold dawn of April, I

confronted a broken man, sobbing like a child, and took a terrible heartless revenge. Why do you cry, I asked. You killed her. And God permitted you."

At the age of 18 Limón not only lost his mother; he also renounced his father and his Catholicism. What was left of his Mexican heritage now? Within a few years he moved to New York City where he discovered his "foster parents"[11] Doris Humphrey and Charles Weidman, and American modern dance.

> "It took the Americans, inheritors of revolutionary and irreverent prejudices against European hegemony, to reject, in toto, the long and revered tradition. Precisely as they had plunged into an unknown and untamed wilderness, going by dead reckoning and oblivious to all obstacles and dangers, so now they had the temerity to abandon the security of the academic tradition and set out to discover or invent their own. It was my good fortune and privilege to observe at first hand the labors of the great revolutionary figures, Doris Humphrey and Charles Weidman."[12]

Limón proudly identified with these Americans who, unlike the Mexicans with their attachment to the European cultural values, were developing a new art form.

> "All the dogma of the ballet was either rejected out of hand, or transformed or adjusted to new urgencies and concepts ... Nobody pointed his toes. The movements of the torso took on a new and crucial importance. Movements of the arms and legs began to be conceived as having their source in the torso, or the organic region. Movement was no longer decorative, but functional. Dance was not pretty, not 'graceful,' nor composed of 'steps.' It had to dig beneath the superficial, and find a powerful beauty, even if it had to be 'ugly' to do so. The elegant stylish contours of the Ballet were twisted and distorted. There were no 'poses,' there were 'patterns' and 'designs' and 'movements.' Away with the debris of a decadent past; an austere, even stark, simplicity was in order.
>
> In justification of their revolutionary fervor and iconoclasm my teachers constantly pointed to the eloquent confirmation manifest in the identical, though much earlier, revolt in the other arts. It was not only illogical but absurd that the dance remain in the nineteenth century when Debussy, Cezanne, Schoenberg, Ibsen and Picasso, to name only a few, had catapulted the other arts into the twentieth. With the fire-brand Isadora Duncan as a guiding beacon, the dancers in America could do no less."[13]

Although some of his early choreographic works excavated material from his Mexican background, they were explicitly created in this new modern dance genre. José Limón was an American modern dancer. The passionate devotion that he exhibited throughout his life to Doris Humphrey seems to enshrine her a surrogate for the mother/Madonna figure he lost when he was eighteen.

Limón's choreographic statements, his dances, supply more clues. His first works were mere études, created under the tutelage of his mentor,

Humphrey, and often had musical titles. Then came *Danzas Mexicanas*, created at Mills College during the summer of 1939, which was derived from images of Mexicans with which he had become haunted. Other than *Chaconne*, it is the only work of his own that he describes in any detail in his unfinished autobiography.

> "I had been planning, for some years, a rather ambitious work, a series of solo dances on a Mexican subject. I had made a number of false starts and had learned in the process what not to do.
>
> I was given the use of a classroom, from which the chairs and desks had been cleared, for my very own, and here I spent my afternoons and evenings, including Saturdays and Sundays ... There were five solos, five symbolic figures from Mexican history: Indio, Conquistador, Peon, Caballero and Revolucionario.
>
> The cruel, heroic and at the same time beautiful story of my native land has held a singular fascination for me. It is never entirely absent from my thinking. I am certain that it has been a strong influence in shaping me into the person I have become. The confrontation of the blood and the culture of the European and the American Indian, resulting in centuries of unremitting conflict, has been resolved within me into something harmonious, into an acceptance and an understanding. I find myself quite at home in any metropolis of the Hispanic world, or a small village in Mexico, and in sympathy with the people, the language and the way of life one finds there. They are important to me: as they made me what I am.
>
> The rare and blessed solitude which I found in the improvised studio that summer gave me, such as I was, to myself. I embarked on the most precarious of journey's, that which we make into one's interior, that 'terra incognita" of the spirit. There was no compass, no starry constellations nor chart to guide me. There was only a blind tropism towards an unknown and distant goal. What I would find there I did not know. All I knew was that I wanted to find who and what I was. For almost ten years I had been pupil, disciple, follower. Now the time had come for me to assume full stature.
>
> My only visitor at the studio during those weeks of sweat and travail was Lionel Novak.[14] ... Sometimes he would improvise. I would jump up and exclaim 'There, that is the sort of thing we need here, or there.' Then I would be alone to continue these introspective forays which were often fruitless and disheartening, but sometimes I would come upon a discovery exciting beyond words, and would experience, as if in recompense for the dull and even despairing hours, such pure rapture that I was suffused with energies and powers I did not know were mine. Living became a sublime adventure. There were moments when I seemed to explode, and the fragile, fleshy envelope and the four confining walls were shattered into oblivion and the only reality was a convulsive, blinding consummation.
>
> I worked like a madman. There is pleasure in remembering that these dances were able to give those who saw them something of what went into their composition. There is pleasure, and even that more rare emotion, satisfaction, in knowing that while making them I grew up."[15]

This dizzying account of Limón's creative process suggests that he was experiencing an intense confrontation and resolution of opposing forces, such as described by Albert Rothenberg as Janusian thinking,[16] and essential to creativity. Rothenberg identifies Janusian thinking as the capacity to conceive and utilize two or more opposite or contradictory ideas, concepts, or images simultaneously. He posits that Janusian thinking occurs during the creative process, which explains the presence and compatibility of seemingly contradictory points of view within a work of art. I find Rothenberg's theory provocative, and see it as an underlying explanation for Limón's genius. He was born into an environment already fraught with contradictions, and these multiplied exponentially as he was growing up in the United States.

In his 1947 work, *La Malinche*, he demonstrates his necessity to resolve these oppositions. The three characters in this work embody aspects of his own feelings about his heritage. The photographer Barbara Morgan said of José: "He said his ancestors came from Spain and that when they came to America, his ancestor, male ancestor, picked out an American Indian woman as mate. And he said he'd always felt guilty that the invading Spanish had taken over. And he really meant it. He said he feels guilty for his ancestors."[17]

It was created for the band of dancers who were to become the nucleus of his first company. The Nordic Lucas Hoving as the "Conquistador" was very like Limón's description of the bullfighter he remembers, "*A man bent on an undertaking gallant, heroic and dangerous.*"[18] "El Indio" is furious and disenfranchised. Pauline Koner as "Malinche" is the peacemaker, who comprehends and loves these two oppositional forces, and is burdened by guilt. She is the traitor to her people, but then, in Limón's version of the story, she joins forces with "El Indio" and together they defeat "the Conquistador". Finally, in the midst of this intense drama we are brought back to reality; this is only a play, an entertainment put on by the band of traveling players for our amusement. The face of Janus is laughing at the same time as it cries. Each role in the ballet seems to represent some aspect of Limón himself, until finally, as the choreographer, he has the last laugh.

Doris Humphrey created several roles for José that portrayed him as a kind of "noble savage." In 1950 Limón first brought his company to Mexico for an immensely successful season. John Martin reported in *The New York Times* that "No artistic event of recent years was reported in numerous Mexican publications, was of such importance there; news magazines gave their covers to pictures of him, the reviews and controversies over some of his repetoire occupied many columns of type, and he and his company were at once figures of national eminence.... The two pieces in his repertory on Mexican or Spanish themes provoked the widest controversy in Mexico. These were *La Malinche* and *Lament for Ignacio Sanchez Mejias*. There were those who fought his interpretation of the former, which is based on a Mexican legend. Objections and oppositions, however, ultimately made no difference, and at last the highly developed taste of the dissenters sensed that this very objectivity was what lifted the creations out of the class of merely native and traditional presentations and into the class of works of art with no national boundaries."[19]

Valentina Castro, who first performed with Limón the following year in Mexico, recalls that controversy. "At that time there were two ways of thinking. There were those who wanted above all to be Spanish, not Mexican; they were against the Mexicans. And there was another way of thinking, of seeking a Mexican nationality with transcendence, with a great Mexican culture. Great painters and musicians like Diego Rivera, Silvestre Siguieros, Blas Galindo and others, belonged to this tendency. They were making Mexican art. And I think *La Malinche* was a ballet which was neither one nor the other . . . When I saw it I understood for the first time that I was a product of the union of both cultures."[20] She went on to explain that her father had been a revolutionary, and she'd been raised to defend the Indian culture, seeing the Spanish as the enemy. The dance affected her deeply, making her recognize her own conflicts. I asked her if she had sensed similar conflicts in José. "No, I never thought he had a conflict; I don't think he did. It was simply that he left Mexico when he was very young, and when he returned, he returned discovering Mexico. I think that he was awed by our culture. He was avid to get to know Mexico. I think that he felt like someone who newly finds, rediscovers, the things that he remembered and that he had always carried in his heart. I don't think he had a conflict, but he did feel a bit like a foreigner. When he arrived in Mexico he became a part of Mexico, and he felt a part of a very rich culture."[21]

Betty Jones remembers how gratified José was about the company's reception. "He went back as a great artist. No one had seen that as of yet in the United States. There was a joy there to be treated that way and to see your picture on Kiosks. And all the great artists were gathering around, the Covarrubias's, and many more artists. This was a very special time for him. In that way it was special. It also probably thrilled him. He remembered his language. He felt comfortable with his language, even having left at seven years old. He felt very comfortable."[22]

In 1951 José was invited to Mexico by the painter Miguel Covarrubias, at that time the director of the dance department of the National Institute of Fine Arts (INFA) and a formidable impressario frequently compared to Diaghelev. Limón came twice during 1951, taught choreography and technique classes at the Institute and created several major new works. This was his first opportunity to work with a large ensemble. *Los Cuatros Soles* had a cast of thirty, which included several totally untrained dancers, as well as a group of weight lifters and acrobats. [23] The dance was large in scale, with a score by Carlos Chavéz and sets and costumes by Covarrubias. It had a libretto, based on pre-Conquest myths, that was put together by the three collaborators, "Mexico's new triumvirate."[24] It was not a masterpiece, but represented an unusual attempt to mount a spectacle approaching the scale of an ancient ritual.

He created three other works for that season, *Antigona* and *Tonantzintla* for the Mexican company, and *Dialogues*, which was a duet for himself and Lucas Hoving. Except for *Antigona*, each was based on some aspect of Mexican history, mythology or architecture. From the memories of those who performed in them, *Tonantzintla* was probably the greatest success. Here is José's story of its genesis:

> "Miguel [Covarrubias] suggested a weekend expedition to Puebla. Miguel knew my predilection for architecture, and particularly for Mexican colonial architecture … I found the Puebla cathedral inspiring as could be, and then Miguel guided me into the smaller chapel to the left of the main altar. I was totally unprepared for what I saw. Here was the fabled 'El Dorado,' that half-dream, half-mirage which maddened the Conquistadores with a lust and frenzy for gold. Walls and ceiling were a mass of scrolls, convolutions and sinuosities, all covered with gold leaf, each elaborate surface at once source and mirror of golden radiance. Under an indescribably wrought canopy stood a sovereign Castilian lady, fair, blue-eyed, robed in a stiff pearl-embroidered robe of sky-blue brocade. She wore a jewel-studded crown. In her arms rested a young prince, like her in regal attire, like her rosy, blue-eyed, blond, and like her, crowned … a beatific vision worthy of the baroque ecstasies of St. Ignatius Loyola, Don Quixote and perhaps Phillip II himself.
>
> "Miguel knew the devastating effect this was having on me. This was sublime theater. Both of us, renegade Catholics, rebels against our backgrounds, were yet as artists enraptured by the supreme presentation. We stood there in silence for a long time. I examined the chapel minutely, drinking in the gorgeous extravagance.
>
> "At last Miguel suggested the resumption of our sight-seeing … after a while we came to a small town. Again our objective was a church, this one called San Juan Ecatepec. The care-taker knew the Covarrubias' and was quite pleasant, unlocking the front portals and ushering us into the cool cavernous interior. This I saw was a replica of the golden chapel. But there was a difference. The baroque style had been subtly modified. It was as grandiose, as sumptuous, but the gold was not as dominant. The indefatigable designs, covering the entire wall space and vaulted ceiling were now radiant with green, blue, red, yellow, but the curved scroll-work did not have the elegance and sophistication of the Puebla Chapel; rather there was a certain naiveté, a slightly provincial element to the total effect. Miguel called my attention to the effigy of the Virgin and Child. They again occupied the place of honor under a canopy, but they were different. They were 'meztizos,' mixed bloods. Black-haired, black-eyed, brunette skinned. Their panoply, still celestial, was no longer entirely Castillian . It was part Indian.
>
> "… We continued our journey. After much driving over roads increasingly primitive and neglected we came to a remote, humble Indian village. Again we headed for the church, and were admitted by a silent Indian caretaker. And here was the utter climax of our expedition. The Chapel of Santa Maria Tonantzintla

was all that we had seen in Puebla and Ecatepec rendered in language and out of the imagination and sensibility of the Indian. His dark genius and ingenuity had transformed the high Baroque into something which had a primitive crude splendor … related to the sacred sculpture of the Toltecs and Aztecs. There were echoes of Teotihuacan. The angels and cherubs, as in the other chapels rampant on the walls and ceiling, were now strange and fantastic figures of the Indian imagination. There were archangels, angels, mermaids and imaginary beasts. The color was violently beautiful, totally, triumphantly uninhibited – crimson, magenta, bright pink, cerulean and turquoise blue, yellow, chartreuse, purple. Only an occasional trace of gold reminded one of the prototype in Puebla.

"The Virgin and Child were Indians, and within the confines of this chapel located in an isolated and forlorn village, the Spanish conquest and centuries of domination seemed nullified.

"Miguel explained once again that the chapel had been built on the spot where stood a temple to the Mother-goddess Tonantzintla, which had been demolished, and its stones used to erect the present chapel. The Virgin Mary and her child and the angels and cherubs and the manner and style of their representation had been taken over by the Indians, and they had created this barbaric splendor.

"The Mother-goddess stood serene, holding her child. But she was surrounded by a joyous pandemonium. Every figure was represented playing some musical instrument, a viol, a trumpet, a guitar, cymbals or drums. Heaven was a place for joy, for music, for celebration. 'Miguel,' I exclaimed, 'the entire place is dancing! Heaven is a huge party!' 'I was hoping you would see that,' he replied. 'Perhaps

José Limón and dancers from the Academia de la Danza Mexicana in *Tonantzintla*.
Photo by Walter Reuter. The Dance Collection, New York Public Library.

you will make us a dance based on what you have seen today. We need it for our season.' "[25]

And so he did, apparently with great charm, to suitably baroque music by Antonio Soler, and with costumes and sets designed by Covarrubias.

> "The little Mermaid, danced with ingenuous charm by Valentina Castro, a very young and talented dancer, was dressed, like her prototype in the ceiling at Tonantzintla, in bright pink and gold, and she held a crimson toy guitar. The angels, again from the chapel, were decked out in regal Aztec panoply, complete with feather head-dresses. The Arch-angel, danced by myself, was a concession to the Spanish influence. Miguel dressed me like a Roman centurion, complete with simulated breast plate and leggings.
>
> In composing this little ballet I kept in mind the style and import of what I had seen at Tonantzintla. The movement was ingenuous, full of child-like wonder and delight. There were motifs derived from Spanish jotas and fandangos. There was formal ornate baroque. Over all was the evocation of a holy pagan joy."[26]

Dialogues was not considered by critics to be as strong a work, although "Mr. Limón's own movement as Montezuma is a new departure for him, the gestures, obviously inspired by Aztec glyphs, imparting a strange two-dimensionality and authenticity to the movement patterns."[27] In it Limón and Hoving were cast in their familiar roles as antagonists, first as Montezuma and Cortez, and later as Juarez and Maximilian, two figures Limón revisited in *Carlota*, the last work he created before his death.

Covarrubias wanted Limón to settle permanently in Mexico. According to John Martin "The honors were topped however by an offer from the government for him to take charge of the general rehabilitation of dance in Mexico along modern lines, with an ample subsidy and on a basis of permanence. This in Mr. Limón's mind was not altogether practicable. For one thing he felt that his career as an artist had been developed in the United States and must be allowed to continue here ... Certainly we in the United States would be grieved to the possible point of making an international incident of it, if what is unquestionably our most important modern dance company were taken away from us."[28]

The following fall Limón returned, this time with Betty Jones as his assistant. They mounted Doris Humphrey's *Passacaglia* for the group and Limón choreographed *Redes* for a large group, and the chamber work *Antigona*, both of which were highly acclaimed. Most of the Mexican dancers that I spoke with remembered *Redes* as being the strongest of the works Limón made in Mexico.

Apparently that first season was a breeding ground for a great deal of major choreography by Mexican choreographers in the next decade. Although several of the dancers Limón worked with had already made their first dances, those I spoke with credited the teachings of Limón and Doris Humphrey, as well as the inspiration derived from their work, as having had a tremendous impact on them. Rosa Reyna remembers that Limón taught a choreography workshop for the first time ever in Mexico, and her *La Manda*, which she developed under Limón's tutelage, was selected by Covarrubias for the opening night performance at Belles Artes, along with the Limón works.[29] She says that in the next two years, over twenty-five dances were created by the dancers who had been in the workshop, including Evelia Beristan, Martha Bracho, Beatriz Flores Castro, Xavier Frances and Elena Noriega. Guillermo Arriaga, who made his first piece in the workshop and two more the following year, says that his signature work, *Zapata*, 1953, would never have been the same if it weren't for the influence of Limón.[30] Farnasio de Bernal was only a beginning dancer during Limón's teaching visits to Mexico, and later went to New York to study with Anna Sokolow and Merce Cunningham, but he still says that it was Limón's passionate and gestural choreography that most influenced him, when he made his *Los Gallos* in 1956.[31]

The opportunity to reminisce with these dancers about their experience working with Limón was a very privileged one; they were all revisiting a very special time in their lives, when they had worked with this extraordinary man, who demanded so much from them, and to whom they felt utterly dedicated. They remembered his sense of spaciousness, of weight, and flow and breath. Some spoke of long and difficult rehearsal hours, or even last minute changes imposed on the choreography by Doris Humphrey. But they all clearly cherish their memories of José.

One of my personal realizations, after teaching dance in Mexico for a few years, and seeing local choreography, was that my body, too, carries Mexican muscle memories. I worked with José for so many years, and absorbed his movement style as my own, without ever realizing how complex the roots were, and I keep discovering more connections.

The story begins and ends with the Mexico that lived, always, within Limón. At the end of his life he still had some last homages and introspections to explore. He made two works, both to be performed in silence. *The Unsung*, which he called a "paean to the heroic defenders of the American Patrimony," was a series of solos for eight men, each exploring a specific native American hero. After a lifetime of seeing El Indio as almost a stock character, an earthy primitive, made bereft of his pagan dignity by cultured invaders, in *The Unsung* he celebrated the singularity of these individuals, and perhaps repossessed a part of himself.

Carlota is a more complex piece to interpret in autobiographical terms. Limón had waited a lifetime to choreograph a dance based on these historical figures. He had discussed making such a piece with Pauline Koner in the forties, and made *La Malinche* instead.[32] In *Dialogues* he had himself danced the part of Benito Juarez, a man he admired so much that he carried his photograph in his make-up kit, and stuck it into his dressing room mirror, where company members saw it and assumed it was his father. But Juarez was not the main character, or even the hero in this work; he was simply part of the situation. Carla Maxwell, current director of the José Limón Dance Company, was cast as the original Carlota.[33] She says that when José began creating the work, he gave her a book to read, *The Cactus Throne*. Limón saw Carlota as a victim of her society and her history. I suspect that he identified more with her situation than with the other characters. She was uprooted from her own culture, and lived among a people she would never fully understand. Possibly he saw her madness as a manifestation of a sane reaction to a world that was intolerable. Whatever the case, we are left with Carlota's last dizzying whirl into grief and madness as Limón's final choreographic effort.

José Limón's name is well known in Mexico. In Culiacán, the city where he was born, there is an arts center, an annual dance festival, and more recently, a street named after him. The national research center for dance in Mexico City is named the CENIDI Danza José Limón. In 1990, when I presented a paper and Master Class in Limón technique at an International Research Conference in Morélia, I was surrounded by young dancers who wanted to know more about Limón, and older ones who wanted to share their memories with me. Lynn Wimmer, Daniel Lewis and Jim May have been greatly appreciated in Mexico as teachers in the Limón style. In some ways I feel that the expressiveness of the style is so natural for Mexican dancers that they have difficulty in defining it. The codification of Graham technique is easier to either embrace or reject. Limón principles, that movement must contain weight and breath, seem so self-evident that after the teachers have gone, the memory that remains is more of the teachers as individuals than of a particular movement approach. And when the present day Limón company performs in Mexico, often the repertory features ballets by choreographers other than Limón. When classic Limón works like *The Moor's Pavane* are performed, by either the National Ballet Company or the Limón Company, those who remember José cannot be satisfied with a substitute. Limón continues to live in Mexico, and he has become a mythic hero.

Notes

1. Excerpt from Limón's hand-written autobiography, probably begun in 1971 or 1972, in the Lincoln Center Library Dance Collection, New York Public Library, NY, gift of Charles Tomlinson, transcribed by Ann Vachon in June, 1996, p. 4.
2. Ibid., p. 3.
3. Ibid., p. 15.

4. Ibid., p. 15.
5. Ibid., pp. 6–7.
6. Ibid., p. 9.
7. Ibid., pp. 10–12.
8. Ibid., p. 20.
9. Ibid., p. 23.
10. Ibid., pp. 23, 24.
11. Ibid., p. 1.
12. Ibid., p. 44.
13. Ibid., pp. 51–52.
14. Lionel Novak was an accompanist and musical director for Humphrey-Weidman, and had composed several works for both Doris Humphrey and Charles Weidman.
15. Limón autobiography, pp. 219–223, transcript pp. 87–88.
16. Albert Rothenberg, "The Process of Janusian Thinking in Creativity," in *The Creativity Question*, edited by Albert Rothenberg and Carl R. Hausman, Duke University Press, Durham, North Carolina, 1976, pp. 312–313.
17. Barbara Morgan, tape recorded interview by Leslie Farlow: November 20, 1985, taken from a transcript in the Lincoln Center Library Dance Collection, New York Public Library, NY.
18. Limón autobiography, p. 12, transcript p. 3.
19. John Martin. *The New York Times*, December 24, 1950.
20. Valentina Castro, interview by author in Mexico City, 1996, videography by Malachi Roth and Aaron Dawley. Translation from the Spanish by Anadel Lynton.
21. Ibid.
22. Betty Jones, interviewed by the author July 7, 1996 at the American Dance Festival, Duke University, videography by Malachi Roth and Aaron Dawley.
23. Fernasio de Bernal, interviewed by the author, Mexico City, August 7, 1992 and Evalia Beristan, on August 5, 1992, with Anadel Lynton as an on-site translator.
24. Walter Terry, "Mexico Produces a New Triumvirate," *Dance Magazine*, June 1951, p. 17.
25. Excerpts from Limón's handwritten article about Covarrubias, date unknown, Lincoln Center Library Dance Collection, New York Public Library, NY, gift of Charles Tomlinson, transcribed by Ann Vachon in August, 1996.
26. Ibid.
27. Louis Horst, "Reviews of the Summer," *Dance Observer*, August 1951, p. 104.
28. John Martin, *The New York Times*, December 24, 1950.
29. Rosa Reyna, interviewed by the author in Mexico City, August 8, 1992, and again April 10, 1996 with videography by Roth and Dawley.
30. Guillermo Arriaga, interviewed by the author in Mexico City, August 6, 1992.
31. Fernasio de Bernal, Interviewed by the author in Mexico City, August 7, 1992.
32. Pauline Koner, interviewed by the author, June 21st, 1996, videography by Roth and Dawley.
33. Carla Maxwell, interviewed by the author, July 15th, 1997, videography by Roth and Dawley.

10

MAZURKAS: ORIGINS, CHOREOGRAPHY, SIGNIFICANCE

Michael Hollander

These are my recollections of *Dances*, which was first presented in August of 1958 at the American Dance Festival at Connecticut College. The work, renamed *Mazurkas* in 1960, was dedicated by José "in honor of Poznan, Wroclaw, Katowice and Warszawa" in reference to his experiences in Poland during a tour of Europe under the US Cultural Exchange Program the previous Fall.[1] Since I performed in the initial production, and participated in the that 1957 tour, I am familiar with the circumstances which had inspired him to create the work.

The audiences we encountered at the outset of the tour, in Paris and in London, were culturally close and familiar with American music and theater, and we assumed they would be highly sympathetic. As it turned out, these were the least supportive of all the audiences we encountered in the nine countries we visited. José described their reactions in a report which he wrote on his return, summarizing the tour: "The opening [in London] was highly inauspicious. The public was small…. The first press critiques were glacial and condescending, often scathing…. There followed [in Paris] what to me seemed the nadir of my artistic fortunes. The Parisian press disliked us intensely and wrote of us with derision and mockery. This kept the public away, of course…. It took courage, for example, to do a good performance on a matinee when the audience present totaled less than the performers, orchestra, and stage crew." (José mentioned in an interview he gave just after writing the report that Ballet Theatre and the New York City Ballet also "had a difficult time" in Paris and that the snub possibly had not been directed at his own work specifically: but at American dance in general.)

The responses in Poland and in Yugoslavia on the other hand were overwhelmingly favorable. In Poland particularly, in each of the four cities we visited – those honored in the dedication – the audiences took us to heart. Catalyzed by Chester Wolenski's greeting in Polish on behalf of the company before each performance, they expressed their admiration for José, our country, and modern dance at every opportunity: in their ovations at curtain calls, and in the exuberant comments they conveyed personally, backstage and outside the stage door. We played to sold-out houses. Also in every respect, they were generous hosts.

As they identified with us, so we identified with them. We empathized with their victimization: first by the Nazis who had destroyed their cities, which lay in ruins still, twelve years after the Second World War; then by the Soviets, who had not only imposed a military presence and subjected them to an incessant barrage of propaganda, blared from loudspeakers in their public squares, but violated their national identity by foisting on their capitol an imperious building complex in the Soviet mold – the "Palace of Culture". We were touched by the beauty of their countryside as it appeared in October, caught in the splendor of what the Poles referred to as their "golden autumn". We were stirred by their devotion to their architectural heritage, exemplified in their laborious and costly restorations of bombed-out historical districts (well before preservation had become a vogue in our own country). And, of course, we admired their institutional support for the arts. In the ballet, for example, concert tickets were very inexpensive and dance classes were free.

One afternoon on a visit to a ballet academy in Poznan run by the State, we were entertained with an informal performance which included a demonstration of Spanish character dancing. On inquiry José learned much to his surprise, that Spanish dance was an important subject of study in Polish schools, a survival of secondary Spanish cultural influences from the past. The event was trivial but symptomatic of the visit; ironically, it was here in Eastern Europe that we found ourselves most at home.

José summarized his reactions in the aforementioned report:

> Poland is an experience which I will not fully grasp, I think, for some time. . . . what I saw and felt as an artist and as a human being is probably the most complex and devastating experience of my life. Against a background of cities still lying eviscerated by the savagery of war, I met human beings of courage, serenity, nobility. There was no rancor, no bitterness. Only a tremendous resolution, a sense of the future. Poland had to be rebuilt. I am in awe of these brave people, of their passionate love for their identity, their tradition, their beautiful survival – but above all, their unspeakable courage.[2]

In the interview which followed, he indicated his intention to pay homage: "The Poles have this tradition of heroic survival. They have a passion for their identity. I found it inspiring. I am going to do a dance about it."[3] This was about two weeks after the tour had ended.

José choreographed *Dances* during the spring and summer of 1958. The same spring he also choreographed *Missa Brevis* for the Juilliard Dance Theater, augmented with Limón company members, in which he paid tribute, separately and more specifically, to the Poles' suffering, faith, and capacity for self-redemption.[4] For the score to *Dances,* Jose selected twelve of the

Mazurkas, a collection by Chopin of stirring peasant dances, vigorous yet tender, many of which he wrote as an expatriate, in Paris. The *Mazurkas* evoked for José the traits he prized so much in the Polish character: valor, grace, simplicity. He may have been drawn as well to something else, which is indicated in the music secondarily: Chopin's attitude of mind in composing the pieces. The image conveyed in Chopin's musical recollection of his homeland is not a simple "picture" but a conception transmuted through the filter of the composer's sentimental consciousness, and it reflects the manner in which he entertained his memories. When José sat at the piano in the studio in New York, black tights, square-necked T-shirt and heavy wool cardigan, towel hung from his neck, picking his way through one or another of the *Mazurkas* as he waited for rehearsal to begin, he must have been thinking back not just to the Polish countryside, but to Chopin himself, speculating on what the composer might have felt like, thinking back on this in Paris a century before.

The inspiration in José's decision to use Chopin's piano music was probably a private concert played one afternoon for the company by Cherny Stepanska (winner of the biennial Warsaw Chopin competition) in an airy salon in the composer's Neoclassical house in Warsaw. We sat in a small group on a cluster of chairs set out informally, looking across the room at the pianist. There was no proscenium intervening between us and the performer, and little distance. The intimacy was highly affecting. We were aware of the pianist as a person, and at the same time we were aware of our selves as individual presences, sensing that our own personal responses to the music were integral to the occasion. This is very different from the circumstances in today's large concert halls, where we are compressed together in a mass and concealed in the dark. The event must have left a deep impression on José in all respects: Chopin's music, the circumstances of the room, and the realization that it was in settings like this that Chopin preferred to perform for his audiences.[5]

José conceived the work as a series of separate dances: five solos, three duets, a quartet, a trio, and a septet for the ensemble. He arranged these in a systematic sequence, using three men and four women, strategically, to introduce asymmetry and to vary the patterns. This format was similar to the one he employed in *Concert* in 1950. The dances were intended to portray various of the Poles' national traits. These traits, however, were imagined in an earlier incarnation, as they might have been embodied in Chopin's time. The dramatizations were subtle, only hinted at, and there was no overt narrative action. The work appeared as if intended for the movement alone, as suggested in its title.

The solos depicted prototypical personae. One of the male figures (Harlan McCallum), for example, was a military gallant, brave, jovial, and courtly. Another (myself) was a reflective consciousness, perhaps

Chopin himself, or some vicarious expatriate like José, listening inwardly, reflecting on memories of his homeland, interrogating them, doubting, judging, acting out the affective content of the musical phrases as if these were movements of thought. The third (Chester Wolenski) was a figure of suffering, anguished, struggling to free himself both from internal and external bondage. This solo, which was performed with great sensitivity, was the centerpiece in the words of one critic, "...the core of what Mr. Limón was trying to say".[6] Ostensibly, José was thinking here of the Poles, in their subjugation by the Soviets, but he had probably enlarged this conception to include a wider set of sufferings: Those of Chopin himself, in his debilitating bouts with pulmonary illness; Jews of the Holocaust, whom the Poles memorialized in their own restorations of Nazi extermination camps such as the one we had visited on the tour at Auschwitz; and Jesus, in his Crucifixion, prompted perhaps by a representation José had seen in a side chapel of the Cathedral of Seville, on Christmas Eve, following the tour's end just before his return home.[7]

The characters in the two women's solos were counterparts to those in the men's. One (Betty Jones), youthful and spirited, gestured provocatively with her wrists and traced intricate patterns on the floor with delicate footwork, all with bite and a hint of bravura. The other (Ruth Currier) was introverted, sweet but sober and uncertain, continually twisting and turning back on herself, head down. Another of the female figures (Lucy Venable) was an austere matriarch to whom José referred playfully in rehearsals as "Mother Poland". The duets portrayed modes of behavior as they occur in amorous relationships. One depicted a couple in innocent accord, moving in unison, matching each other step for step, each soul reflected in the other's. Another, a pair out of phase, frustrated by some irreconcilable class or personal division; the first offering, beseeching; the other parrying and turning aside, still bound by an inviolable code. José developed these various personae by opportunistically exploiting propensities in each of our own personalities, manifest in the natural qualities of our movements. He was certainly familiar with these propensities, having coached us day in and day out for years in class and in rehearsal. Indicative of this interdependence between dancer and work which emerged in the choreographic process, Sarah Stackhouse, in reconstructing *Mazurkas* from video a few years ago, chose to identify the various roles by referring in each case to the name of the original dancer.

The compositional aspects of the choreography were highly developed at all levels, from the overall organization which was tied to the rigorous formal structure of the music, to the movement vocabulary which reflected, in spirit, the stylized patterns and steps of mazurka dance forms. The men's feet, for example, booted in military fashion, were and accorded prominence. At various times, their lower legs stood forward assertively, knees bent and heels rotated to the front; or their metatarsal in "half-toe" position with heels lifted, pressed hard against the floor, stepping down or pounding; or the full soles of their feet flexed upward, heels jutting defiantly out. The interplay between these two aspects of the work, the compositional structure and the dramatic content, although not developed consistently, was an essential feature. It evoked allegorically the constraint which social convention, symbolized here by the mazurka-like patterns, imposes upon individual behavior. Although passions erupted, decorum prevailed. A tragic and much more overt statement of this same theme is apparent in *The Moor's Pavane*.

The movement at the core of the dance, the basic material from which both the drama and the formal patterns were created, was quite beautiful. The dance was classical in its sense, lucid and economical in its means. The forms of the gestures, the configurations of the phrases in which these gestures were combined, and the larger sections – the introductory statements, developmental passages, and conclusions – were composed with considerable craft. Every gesture was impelled by something deep within the dancer; arms, legs, chest, hips, knees, feet, were motivated extensions of the inner self, instruments of being. This was fundamental in José's work and one of his great contributions. It stands against the depersonalization of the human body, whether for the sake of design, as can happen in ballet when limbs are used to form abstract linear configurations, or for the sake of novelty, as occurs in certain more recent modern dance.

José's choreography reflected his understanding and appreciation of the music as a pianist. The fluctuations of mood depicted in the various characterizations, for example, were tied both to the transformations which occurred in musical themes when they were reiterated in major and minor keys, and to the rhythmic cadences. In this way, the phrasing of the movement mediated the musical and the dramatic structures, correlating them intelligently and at the same time respecting the integrity of each. It was not enough, however, for José to realize this interrelation between music and dance in practical terms, he wanted also to present theatrically. For this reason he placed the piano on the stage and provided a prologue, performed in silence, in which the dancers arrived arm in arm, in twos and threes, as if to attend a salon concert, and acknowledged the pianist with a nod or bow. The piano, an obtrusive physical presence which jutted into the performing area, served palpably to invoke the presence of the composer. The intimacy between musician and dancers on the stage reenacted the situation of the concert in Chopin's house and recalled the spirit of reciprocity which prevailed there. In *Dances*, José had imagined Chopin's *Mazurkas* as a "gift", to the dancers and he intended the dances as offerings in appreciation. José had

Mazurkas. Dancers from left to right: Michael Hollander, Betty Jones, Lola Huth, Lucy Venable, Harlan McCallum, Ruth Currier and Chester Wolenski. Photo by Willaim Vandivert. The Dance Collection, New York Public Library.

enacted this same relationship between dancer and musician previously both in *Concert* and in *Chaconne*. Although the theme may have been suggested by an experience in Poland, this was not its source.

Mazurkas represented, in several respects, a significant if not seminal development in José's career as an artist. For one thing, he had excluded himself from the dance, implying that he was now prepared, at fifty, to diminish his participation as a performer. He had absented himself similarly three years before from *Scherzo*, but in that case his purpose was to present a demonstration of male dancing, in and of itself. In addition, he had expanded the cast to include younger members of the company. Although he had done this in *The Traitor*, for example, and in *The Emperor Jones*, in this instance, for the first time he had treated these performers as soloists and not as an ensemble. This returned to the choreographic format based on the interaction of a few discrete voices as it occurs in chamber music, identified with the previous "core" company, consisting essentially of Ruth, Betty, Letitia Ide, Pauline Koner, Lucas Hoving, and José himself, and seen typically in *The Exiles, The Visitation, The Moor's Pavane* and Doris Humphrey's *Night Spell*.

The work set another precedent in its use of Romantic music. Up to this point José, following Doris' example, had drawn primarily either on Baroque composers such as Bach and Vivaldi, or on various 20th century composers including Schoenberg, Barber, Villa-Lobos and Schuller. His only prior involvement with the 19th century had been satiric, as in *Don Juan Fantasia*, which used Liszt's composition of the same name. José's shift marked a significant turn, but what had changed was not his convictions about music so much as his willingness to act on these convictions as an artist. This was apparent in a remark he had made on an earlier occasion, during a discussion of accommodations to rehearsal schedules necessitated by religious holidays: "If there is a God, it is Chopin and Bach".

His decision to use Chopin's music involved an important development in his choreographic vision. José's essential concern as an artist was to invent heroic prototypes appropriate to life in the modern world. One of the mythic figures he had conceived in *La Malinche* was a Mexican folk-hero, part modern peasant, part Pre-Columbian: earthbound, stolid, unyielding. Another, developed both in conjunction with Doris in *Lament for Ignacio Sanchez Mejias*, and independently in *The Moor's Pavane*, was a courtly Spaniard: proud, generous, impassioned. A third, seen in *The Exiles* and in *The Visitation*, was a biblical patriarch: humble, devout, innocent. In *Mazurkas*, José created a new heroic model, based on early 19th century European aristocracy, who upholds the ideals of Neoclassicism, tempered with the sentiments of Romanticism. This figure represents the end of the "past", the final moment in modern Western history, just before the full onslaught of industrial civilization, when noble individuality, moral purpose, and grandeur of character still seemed a possibility. José, as a modernist, was concerned with this heroic ideal as an example of universal traits, not in any literal historical sense.

In *Mazurkas*, this aristocratic type is embodied in the dancers' "carriage". The rib cage is expanded, breath drawn into the lungs, and lifted out of the lower trunk, drawing the frame of the body upward with it; chin, neck and shoulders are pulled away from each other, up, down and out, forming an airy arch of space between. The type was embodied also in the phrasing of the movement. Each sequence of gestures had a distinct overall configuration, formed of graduated rises and falls. Typically, the torso would be borne upward in a series of breathy suspensions, hung precipitously in the air, then brought to a gentle subsiding rest. In all, a staunch spirit prevailed, softened here and there by sentimental turns. José's strategic selection of younger members of the company, rather than himself, Hoving, and Koner, would seem to have been essential to this stylistic conception.

Little if any of this was apparent to audiences at the original performances: they enjoyed the work and applauded graciously but were not profoundly moved. Nor were the critics: Walter Terry, for example, described the piece *in The New York Herald Tribune* as "a suite of Polish flavored *numbers* [italics mine] ... with one or two exceptions lighthearted of spirit", and commented: "Truthfully it's all rather thin and dreary"; P. W. Manchester noted: "All choreographers are entitled to make an occasional mistake and this was one of Limón's rare slip-ups".[8]

It is hard to understand why the reviews were unsympathetic. Certainly, the dance was uneven in quality and too long, and several of the sections needed to be developed, but these are secondary issues and one would imagine that the critics would have been able to see past them and glimpse what lay beyond. Possibly they had been misled by the trappings: the music which on the surface could be linked with romantic ballet, and the costumes which were too literally ornamented with braided silver swags and tassels across the chest and thick piping at the collar of the men's jackets, which gave the work a "historical" cast. This was uncharacteristic. Limón costumes, since *Dialogues* and *Tonantzintla* in 1951, had been plain and unornamented, even when it was necessary to evoke the dress of some particular period. (In this instance, they had been designed by Lavina Nielsen, not Pauline Lawrence Limón.) Focusing on these extrinsic features, the critics might well have assumed that the work was intended as a light entertainment – not recognizing that it represented a significant extension of José's enterprise as a dancer and choreographer, or that it retrieved romantic musical imagery from the associations with fantasy, developed in most traditional ballet, and restored to it some of its moral content. The virtues of José's inventive theatrical format, the piano placed on stage, and his use of Chopin, however, were not lost on others like Jerome Robbins, who seems to have drawn direct inspiration from *Dances* for his own ballet, *Dances at a Gathering*.

Considered in retrospect, the premiere performances of *Mazurkas* marked a curious juncture in the history of modern dance in the late 1950's. Anticipating the next phase of his career, José had returned to an earlier choreographic format, revamped with an expanded younger cast, and created a dance which although innovative and adventurous appeared peripheral, if not regressive, to the main thrust of his work. Significantly, at the same time, Merce Cunningham had arrived on the scene at New London both as a teacher at the School of the Dance and as a performer and choreographer at the American Dance Festival. From our present vantage, Cunningham's appearance signified the radical programmatic reorientation in modern dance which was to occur with his own rise to prominence in the following decade – in essence, a rejection of the idealism and positive belief at the root of José's work. Ordinariness would be prized over heroism; detachment over passion; wit over weight; chance over committed choice. José and Merce, sharing the stage that August, were two currents in dance, both displaced from the center, passing in opposite directions: José drifting somewhat nostalgically from the 20th century back in time; Merce venturing ahead, beyond the familiar pale of current practice.

Following its premiere, *Mazurkas* was performed in practice clothes, upgraded somewhat with a few token embellishments. José explained that the costumes had been lost in a fire but whether this actually occurred is not certain. After 1958 *Mazurkas* was presented six times in this country and taken on tour to South America and then abandoned. Other of José's promising works during this period, *Don Juan Fantasia* and *Blue Roses* had also been cut prematurely instead of being revised and developed in order to make room in the crowded repertory for new pieces.

The dance was much admired by members of the original and later companies and reconstructed in part or in its entirety by three: Betty Jones in Honolulu in the early 1980's with an informally assembled cast; Ann Vachon with her own company in 1988, and Sarah Stackhouse with members of the Limón Company in 1992, at which time it was restored to the Company repertory.[10] *Dances* is preserved in three videotaped versions: one, of the original cast in rehearsal clothes without music, blurred and speeded up; one, of Ann's ensemble in costume; and one, of the 1992 company in practice clothes.[11] The work is preserved also in the memories of everyone privileged to have performed in it.

* * *

All these events took place 40 years ago, and my memories are highly selective. I remember little specifically of what José said during rehearsals, but I recall vividly what he looked like and sounded like as he indicated his intentions – his gestures, facial expressions, and the tone of his voice. By the same token, I remember little of my movement, but I recall exactly what I felt like as I danced, and the images I constructed to help me perform the role the way he intended. I recall also what I thought about the *Mazurkas* from a critical stand point and how I understood its relation to José's other dances. I never knew, however, what it looked like to audiences. It was not until 1992, in Sarah Stackhouse's revival, that I actually saw it performed in its entirety from the other side of the proscenium. Because I stopped dancing a few months after the premiere to change my carrer and lost contact altogether, not just with the company but with the world of modern dance – the recollections have remained frozen, stored in a time capsule. If they are dim, they are at least, from a historical point of view, original.

The only direct evidence I can offer of José's thinking is a report in the form of an open letter which he sent to company members and other concerned parties. It was written January 6, 1958, two weeks after the last performance of the tour in Oporto, Portugal which took place just before Christmas in 1957. Also there is a transcription of an interview "re trip to Europe for ANTA", given three days later, the interviewing party unidentified. Copies of both are housed in the Collection of The Limón Dance Foundation.

I wish to thank several members of the original and later casts, Betty Jones, Lucy Venable, Chester Wolenski, Ann Vachon, James Payton, and Sarah Stackhouse, whose contributions filled important gaps, added valuable insight, and brought a number of my misconceptions to my attention. Norton Owen, Institute Director of the José Limón Dance Foundation, was also very helpful in providing documentary data.

The program listing for the premiere, August 15, 1957, was as follows:

> **DANCES** ... (Mazurkas) Chopin
> (in honor of Poznan; Wr[o]claw; Katowice; and Warszawa)
> HOWARD LEBOW, Pianist
> JOSÉ LIMÓN, Choreography
> Entrance ... ENTIRE COMPANY
> Duet (op. 41, no. 1) ... LOLA HUTH, CHESTER WOLENSKI
> Solo (op. 30, no. 2) ... BETTY JONES
> Solo (op. 41, no. 3) ... HARLAN McCALLUM
> Trio (op. 33, no. 2) ... MICHAEL HOLLANDER,
>   CHESTER WOLENSKI, HARLAN McCALLUM
> Solo (posthumous, A. minor) ... RUTH CURRIER

Solo (op. 59, no. 2)...MICHAEL HOLLANDER
Quartet (op. 56, no. 1)...RUTH CURRER, LUCY VENABLE,
   LOLA HUTH, BETTY JONES
Solo (op. 17, no. 4)...CHESTER WOLENSKI
Duet (op. 30, no. 4)...RUTH CURRIER, HARLAN McCALLUM
Septet (op. 56, no. 3)...ENTIRE COMPANY
Duet (op. 59, no. 1)...BETTY JONES, MICHAEL HOLLANDER
Finale (op. 30, no. 3)...ENTIRE COMPANY
LAVINA NIELSEN: Costumes
THOMAS SKELTON: Lighting

Notes

1. The Cultural Exchange Program provided that the various artists be sent abroad as "cultural ambassadors" both to ease tensions which had developed during the cold war and to develop cultural bonds which could pave the way for political rapprochements, as José had been counseled, "to make friends through our art" (Report 6 January 1958, p. 2, Collection of Limón Dance Foundation). The Limón Company had traveled to South America several years before under the same program and had been requested to serve again. In the interview José proudly described, several incidents in Yugoslavia in which he felt he had succeeded in the mission. (Interview "re trip to Europe for ANTA", by an unidentified party, 9 January 1958, p. 6, typewritten transcription, Collection of Limón Dance Foundation.) [2]   Report, p. 3.
2. Report, p. 3.
3. Interview. p. 2. José was moved also by his experiences in Yugoslavia, but was not inspired artistically. This was possibly because the country, unlike Poland, was culturally diffuse and lacked a cohesive national identity.
4. In discussing his visit to the cathedral in Seville further along in the interview, José repeated his intention to choreograph a dance. This time, however, it might have been in reference to *Missa Brevis*: "In the ruins of Poland I found a dance. I was in Spain from the 23rd of December to January 2nd. On Christmas Eve, [I] went to Mass in the cathedral in Seville. The Gothic cathedral is tremendous, one of the most soaring monuments to the human spirit. But the mass was an empty ritual. A mass is an act of faith. I shall make a dance which is an act of faith. It will have nothing to do with religion as we know it commercially." (Interview, p. 8)
5. José did not refer to the Chopin concert in the report probably because it was written as a formal assessment of the tour and not as a record of his personal experiences
6. Doris Hering. The date and source were missing from the copy on file at the Institute of the Limón Foundation.
7. Interview, p. 8. José documents this experience in some personal notes ("In a chapel of the Cathedral of Sevilla, Christmas Eve 1957", 4pp., Dance Collection, New York Public Library for the Performing Arts.) The notes which are highly revealing of his spiritual and moral convictions, were brought to my attention by Ann Vachon.
8. The Terry review was published August 18, 1958. The source and date of the P. W. Manchester review were detached from the copy available at the Institute of the Limón Foundation.
9. José wrote, typically, in the report: "I have...a strong faith in our art, and what it represents, its power, its vitality, its validity and its sincerity as a voice speaking for us as Americans of the twentieth century." (Report, p. 1)

10. Ann Vachon had an additional personal interest in reconstructing the dance. Her father, John Vachon, a photojournalist who later worked for *Look Magazine,* had visited Poland in 1946, just after the war to document living conditions for the United Nations Relief and Rehabilitation Agency. Ann revisited Poland in order to retrace her father's steps, aware that the company had travelled the same path earlier. Ann describes her venture in the "Afterword" of a book on her father's photography, *Poland, 1946* (Smithsonian Institution Press, 1995).

11. All three videotapes are housed in the Collection of the Limón Dance Foundation.

11

THE 1954 LIMÓN COMPANY TOUR TO SOUTH AMERICA: GOODWILL TOUR OR COLD WAR CULTURAL PROPAGANDA?

Melinda Copel

In 1949, with the detonation of a nuclear device by the Soviet Union, the world hung in an uneasy balance between two superpowers, the United States and the Soviet Union, each of which now had the capability to initiate a nuclear war. The specter of a nuclear holocaust led both superpowers to adopt a policy of military containment. The fear of communism in the United States led to the interrogation and blacklisting of American citizens and to censorship in the arts, the media, and academia. It also led to the governmental exportation of American arts and culture with the intent of winning over foreign intellectuals to American capitalism and, thus, stemming the spread of Communism worldwide.

On November 19 of 1954, José Limón and his company of dancers set out on a hastily arranged tour to South America. The tour was the first to be sponsored by the newly formed Performing Arts International Exchange Program which was administered by the American National Theatre and Academy (ANTA) under the auspices of the U.S. State Department. President Eisenhower authorized the use of emergency funds to finance the trip as funds had not yet been allocated for the newly formed program.[1] It was the first time a modern dance company had received financial support from the government for a foreign tour. The company was scheduled to perform in four cities – Rio de Janeiro and São Paulo, Brazil; Montevideo, Uruguay; and Buenos Aires, Argentina.[2] The Buenos Aires performances were canceled at the last minute by the local organizer.[3] The State Department planned the Limón company's Rio de Janeiro appearances to coincide with the Rio Economic Conference and the Montevideo performances to coincide with the annual meeting of UNESCO.[4] The company was scheduled to return on December 21; however, because of the canceled engagement in Buenos Aires, they actually returned on December 15.

The 1954 tour was set against the backdrop of American Cold War politics. The execution of Julius and Ethel Rosenberg on June 19, 1953 was still fresh in the minds of Americans (and the world). Convicted in 1951 of conspiracy to commit espionage, the Rosenbergs maintained their innocence to the end, even though a confession would have spared their lives. Historians are still divided on the question of their probable involvement in a conspiracy to pass information on the production of the atomic bomb to the Russians. The evidence against Ethel Rosenberg has been particularly called into question.[5] The executions, which orphaned the Rosenberg's two young sons, caused a world outcry. French philosopher Jean-Paul Sartre called them, "a legal lynching that has covered a whole nation in blood."[6] The convictions fueled the activities of the House Committee on Un-American Activities (HUAC), a congressional committee established to investigate activities of American citizens that were deemed dangerous to the United States government. HUAC questioned American citizens about their ties to the Communist Party and their loyalty to the United States government. Allegations were often based on the flimsiest of evidence.[7] Membership in communist organizations or organizations which were considered to be communist fronts, friendships with communist sympathizers, production of literary or art works considered to support communist ideals or to present an unfavorable picture of Americans or American culture, and expression of ideas which were thought to be in sympathy with communist ideals were reason enough to be called before the committee. This committee was chaired by Senator Joseph McCarthy from 1950 through 1954. Those called before the committee were pressured to implicate or to name others as Communists or potential security risks. Being called before the committee often resulted in the blacklisting of artists, writers, educators and free thinkers. Many lost their jobs or could no longer find markets for their creative work. Members of the Screen Actors Guild, employees of major television networks, and employees of many colleges and universities were required to sign anti-Communist loyalty pledges in order to keep their jobs. The State Department removed from libraries books and paintings which had been created by "any controversial persons, Communists, fellow travelers, et cetera."[8] An atmosphere of censorship and conformity prevailed. 1954 was also the year that McCarthy accused officials of the U.S. Army and the Senate of being Communists. This proved to be his downfall. Anti-McCarthy sentiment had been growing in the country because of unfavorable publicity from the hearings; McCarthy had at last pushed too far. In December of 1954, McCarthy was censured by the Senate for "contempt of a Senate subcommittee, misconduct, abuse of certain Senators, and insults to the Senate."[9]

Several notable events of 1954 typified the Cold War culture. It was during this year that the United States and Canada announced plans to build the Distant Early Warning (DEW) system across the northern part of the continent to warn North American citizens of imminent attack by the Soviets.[10] It was the year that Congress voted to add the phrase "one nation under God" to the Pledge of Allegiance, at the suggestion of Reverend George M. Docherty, to distinguish the ideology of the United States from that of the Soviet Union.[11] Congress also passed the Communist Control Act which deprived American citizens who belonged to the Communist Party of basic civil rights.[12] In 1954, the Supreme Court decided the landmark case of Brown vs. the Board of Education which mandated the desegregation of American public schools; this decision drew charges that the court had succumbed to Marxist thinking.[13] It was within this atmosphere that the State Department selected the José Limón company to promote goodwill and present a positive image of American culture and the American way of life under capitalism to the people of South America.

The United States, as a global superpower, held a position of economic and political power superior to that of the Latin American countries. The economy and further economic development of Latin America depended on the United States. In addition, the United States provided markets for raw materials and agricultural products, investment capital for Latin American businesses through private investors, and manufactured goods to Latin America. At the same time, Latin America was of great political and economic interest to the United States. It was considered a region vital to the U.S. goal of preventing the spread of Communism. The low standard of living of many Latin American citizens, exploitative working conditions, and the disparity between rich and poor were seen as factors that made these nations vulnerable to Communist takeover. They prompted Harold Stassen, Director of the Foreign Operations Administration, to warn that, if the U.S. did not work to improve economic conditions in Latin American nations, "the impetus of social justice will be seized by the Communists and used to promote their system."[14] Thus, economic stability and improved economic conditions in Latin America were seen as matters of National Security. Latin America also possessed large quantities of undeveloped natural resources which were of particular interest to American investors.

The Rio Economic Conference, which was to be held in Quitandinha, Brazil (about 40 miles from Rio) beginning on November 22, 1954, the same day the Limón company opened in Rio, was of great importance to the United States. President Eisenhower appointed a Sub-Cabinet Committee to review U.S. economic policies with regard to Latin America and to formulate policies and position statements for the upcoming conference. Differences of opinion concerning the proper positions to be taken at Rio surfaced among different factions of the committee, in particular, the Foreign Operations Administration (FOA), the U.S. Treasury Department, and the State Department. The FOA favored a more pro-active economic position toward Latin America that would encourage development and, thereby, raise the standard of living among the Latin American peoples.

> FOA believes that the U.S. economic policy toward Latin America is inadequate and that from that inadequacy are coming and will continue to come very serious political and security problems; therefore it is very important that the U.S. develop a new, adequate policy.[15]

This position was seen as imperative to preventing the spread of Communism in this part of the world.

Latin American countries wanted three things to come from the Rio conference. The first was a commitment by the United States to give them treatment equal to that given in other areas of the world in the development of financing; the second was the formation of an Inter-American Bank, to be financed partially by U.S. capital, which would make development loans. The third was the creation of a minimum price support to be paid for Latin American commodities and raw materials.[16]

The Sub-Cabinet Committee balked at formulating positions that would meet the Latin American requests. The issue of providing U.S. capital for a new bank and the issue of price supports were particular sticking points. The committee preferred to place an emphasis on capital coming from private sources. Some officials feared that U.S. government financed loans to Latin America might usurp investment opportunities for private investors. As final positions for the conference were being formulated, some members of the committee expressed concern that the positions to be presented were inadequate and would be received negatively by the Latin Americans. The fiscally conservative Treasury Department, however, insisted that the formation of an Inter-American Bank was not sound economic policy, and that the Latin Americans must be urged to seek private financing.[17]

On October 11, 1954, the Latin American Working Group of the Operations Coordinating Board of the National Security Council issued a top secret report which stated that the proposed positions fell short of carrying out established National Security Council policies. The report urged that the positions be revised to take a more positive stand towards U.S. assistance to Latin American economic development.[18] The Sub-Cabinet Committee stressed the importance of presenting the positions in as positive a light as possible if the Rio Conference was to be a success. Assistant Secretary of State Holland had gone to South America several weeks before the conference to feel out responses to the positions the U.S. was intending to take and to engage in diplomatic groundwork. The U.S. State Department, realizing that the positions to be presented at the Rio Conference were going to be problematic, acknowledged the need to meet with Latin American delegates individually to persuade them to accept the U.S. positions. Ultimately, the positions taken at the conference fell short of those requested by the Latin Americans.

On October 19, Robert Schnitzer of the International Exchange Program and José Limón met to begin arranging the details of the Limón company tour. Notes from Limón's appointment book and diary indicate that Schnitzer had called Limón the week prior to the October 19 meeting to discuss the tour.[19] On October 28, Schnitzer began sending out letters to free the Limón company dancers from other performing engagements. In these letters he stated that the State Department had specifically requested that the Limón company make a brief tour of South America at the time of the Rio conference and a conference in Montevideo (the UNESCO conference). He called the project one "of major importance to our country's international relations."[20]

Limon's diary entries express a sense of elation, excitement, and pride about the upcoming tour, as well as some understanding of its diplomatic aspects. He writes of preparations for the tour, "this, to us, fabulous project," and states that the Limón company repertory will be examined and programs planned specifically for South American audiences.[21] His entry of October 29 clearly states his feelings at being chosen to represent the United States.

> ANTA, American National Theatre and Academy. At last something more than an idea or a name. Eisenhower requesting, and authorizing from Congress, five million to send U.S. culture and know-how abroad, to make friends and acquaint the world with other fascets [sic] of our life than the brilliant and stupendous material accomplishments. I am happy and proud and honored to be chosen as an emissary. I will try to be worthy.[22]

It is my contention that the U.S. State Department sought to stack the deck by engaging the talents of a man who was sure to win over the hearts of the Latin American people. José Limón became the first artist to receive funds under the State Department's newly formed International Exchange Program; however, the precedent for using artists and their work to fight Communism and to present a selective view of American culture had already been set in the post-World War II era. Much later, *The New York Times* would expose a CIA covert operation which had funneled hundreds of thousands of dollars into various cultural organizations including the Whitney Museum Trust.[23] Thomas Braden, who left the CIA in 1954, acknowledged his part in operations designed to fight Communism and lessen Communist influence by supporting the work of American artists around the world.

> I remember the enormous joy I got when the Boston Symphony Orchestra won more acclaim for the U.S. in Paris than John Foster Dulles or Dwight D. Eisenhower

could have bought with a hundred speeches. And then there was *Encounter*, the magazine published in England and dedicated to the proposition that cultural achievement and political freedom are interdependent. Money for both the orchestra's tour and the magazine's publication came from the CIA, and few outside the CIA knew about it.[24]

The Museum of Modern Art (MOMA) was also involved in the scheme to fight Communism. MOMA provided cultural materials for the Library of Congress, the Office of War Information, and Nelson Rockefeller's Office of the Coordinator of Inter-American Affairs. MOMA shipped nineteen art exhibits around Latin America during the Cold War.[25]

The aesthetic of Abstract Expressionism was used to promote the ideology of "freedom" in the U.S. at a time when civil rights were actually being curtailed in the U.S. as a result of McCarthyism and Cold War politics.[26] It was important to present a picture of the individual freedom of American artists to the rest of the world even as many artists in this country were being blacklisted for their political beliefs or the alleged political content of their work.

> CIA and MOMA cultural projects could provide the well-funded and more persuasive arguments and exhibits needed to sell the rest of the world on the benefits of life and art under capitalism.... CIA sought to influence the foreign intellectual community and to present a strong propaganda image of the United States as a "free" society as opposed to the "regimented" communist bloc.[27]

In January of 1955, only six weeks after the Limón tour to South America, and at the request of the State Department, violinist Isaac Stern was sent on a cultural mission to Iceland under the same International Exchange Program which supported the Limón tour. Stern's visit to Iceland followed that of a Russian delegation of musicians and dancers. Speaking of his previous ten years touring the globe, Isaac Stern affirmed the world view of Americans as materialistic and acknowledged the power of the arts to bridge cultural gaps.

> We had given concerts around the world and had seen potential friends of the United States alienated by the nation's material wealth. The language of the arts, which could create better understanding, was being ignored by our country in areas where music, painting and literature were regarded more highly than refrigerators and automobiles as evidence of civilization. [28]

Apparently Stern was unaware of the extent to which the CIA and the State Department were already exploiting the ability of the arts to reap political benefits. It is clear that the CIA and the U.S. State Department considered the exportation of American arts and culture to have a beneficial effect on U.S. foreign relations.

José Limón constituted an ideal choice as an artist/diplomat. Limón, who was born in Mexico, had proven extremely popular in his visits to Mexico City in 1950 and 1951. His Hispanic background provided common ground with the Latin Americans. In addition, the Limón company repertory included several works on Spanish or Mexican themes, *Lament for Ignacio Sánchez Mejías, Ritmo Jondo*, and *La Malinche*; and several dances inspired by biblical themes, *The Exiles, The Visitation*, and *The Traitor*. These dances could be expected to receive an enthusiastic reception from the largely Catholic and Hispanic South American audiences. Also, the U.S. support of a Hispanic artist gave the appearance of a valuing by the U.S. government of Hispanic contributions and culture. In 1954, Limón's place in American dance was well-established. His company was one of the foremost modern dance companies in the country. John Martin had called Limón, "the finest male dancer of his time."[29] The choreographic genius of Doris Humphrey, Limón's mentor and artistic director of the Limón company, also contributed to its success. The strong humanistic content of Limón's dances presented a sympathetic view of American culture. Limón's work was situated in the already established field of American modern dance; he was not a part of the fledging dance avant-garde which was beginning to explore new directions.[30] His work was readily understood and unlikely to offend, confuse, or mystify his audiences.

The tour was publicized as a goodwill gesture designed to familiarize citizens of foreign countries with American art forms; however, Limón's personal correspondence attests to the diplomatic nature of the tour.[31] Sally Hope, wife of U.S. delegate to the UNESCO conference Henry Hope, wrote to Limón welcoming him to Montevideo on behalf of the delegation. In her letter, Mrs. Hope informed Limón that the U.S. delegation had invited members of each of the delegations to the UNESCO conference as well as diplomats and government officials to the Limón company performances which she called, "the crowning event of the cultural presentations."[32] In a letter to Doris Humphrey, Limón writes that the company has been very busy with, among other things, "social and semi-political or diplomatic obligations...this has been a very important thing to do both artistically and ideologically."[33] In addition to the scheduled performances, an extra performance was added in Rio for the labor unions at which many important government officials were present, including the Labor Minister, who was photographed with Limón after the performance for both the press and the local television station.[34] The company gave a lecture demonstration at The Museum of Modern Art in Rio, Limón speaking in Spanish and the company demonstrating the technique and sections of the repertory. Limón was interviewed on Rio television and, later the same evening, he was invited to a gathering of local critics, journalists, and columnists to address their questions.[35]

Company member Alvin Schulman states that the purpose of the tour was to have the troupe represent the culture of North America and act as an ambassador for modern dance. Schulman also speaks of the ability of art to present a view of American culture that was able to counter the perception of Americans as greedy and materialistic.

> Here was a new strange audience once again saying, "Show us!" The pressure to perform is at anytime enough to rack one's nerves, but how much more so when you have to come across for an audience that (only too well aware of the wonderful automobiles and kitchen-gadgets we Americans produce) is waiting eagerly on the other side of the curtain to see what kind of culture we are capable of.[36]

Limón's art served as a powerful tool for countering Communist attacks on American culture and for representing our culture in a more positive light. Speaking of a later Limón company State Department sponsored tour to Latin America in 1960, Percy Warner, the U.S. Consulate in Porto Alegre, Brazil reiterated the importance of these tours to U.S. foreign relations.

> The themes offered and their performance by the Limón group showed a humanism and spiritual depth which is not often associated with the culture of the United States to the extent that it is known in these parts. Thus, to an audience of intellectual leaders and opinion-formers whom we usually have difficulty in reaching in such a way, this Limón performance was an impressive offset to the insidious and constant efforts to portray the U.S. as a heartless and materialistic community without humanistic sentiments or culture.
>
> It is certain that the affair had an important and profound impact at a time when it is [sic] especially needed.[37]

Limón seems to have served the State Department well as an ambassador of American goodwill. Similar testimony of his effectiveness during the 1957 State Department sponsored tour to Europe is affirmed by a story relating Limón's success at winning over the Communist Mayor of a town in Yugoslavia. Impressed by the company's performance, the Mayor invited the company to a reception and expressed his desire to see the performance again. Ecstatic United States Information Agency personnel procured seats for the Mayor. One of the USIA agents explained to Limón that the Mayor had previously refused to meet with Americans. Limón had paved the way for friendly relations with a Communist official in politically crucial Eastern Europe.[38] In 1964, Limón received the prestigious Capezio Dance Award. It was presented to him by Lucius Battle, Assistant Secretary for Educational and Cultural Affairs for the State Department. The award honored Limón not only for his contributions to American dance, but also for his effectiveness as a cultural ambassador.[39]

In his autobiography, written at the end of his life, Limón professes little interest in American politics. He was far more concerned with the atrocities committed during the Spanish Civil War by the Fascist regime of General Franco. Limón was particularly saddened by the killing of Spanish poet Federico Garcia Lorca. Unfortunately, his autobiography ends with the year 1942, so it gives little insight into Limón's view of Cold War politics.[40]

The Limón company departed from New York City on November 19, 1954 and arrived in Rio de Janeiro where they performed from November 22–29. The second week they performed in São Paulo, Brazil from November 30–December 5, and the third week in Montevideo, Uruguay from December 7–12. The Montevideo performances coincided with the last week of the UNESCO annual meeting that was held in Montevideo from November 12–December 11. The company was scheduled to perform from December 15–22 in Buenos Aires, Argentina, but the engagement was canceled at the last minute. Alvin Schulman claims that the performances were canceled because the Argentinean organizer did not want to present the company during the hot season.[41] It is possible that this was a polite excuse and that the Buenos Aires performances were canceled for political reasons. The Rio Conference had ended December 2 and the Latin American countries had not been entirely satisfied with the U.S. positions or with the vote of the U.S. delegation on certain crucial issues.

Twelve dances were presented on the tour: *Ode to the Dance, The Moor's Pavane, La Malinche, The Visitation*, and *Vivaldi Concerto Grosso*, choreographed by Limón, and *Night Spell, Ritmo Jondo, Ruins and Visions, Day on Earth, Story of Mankind*, and *Variations and Conclusion from New Dance*, choreographed by Doris Humphrey. Lucas Hoving performed his comic duet, *Satyros*, with his wife, Lavina Nielsen.[42] Pauline Koner was to have performed her solo, *Cassandra*, but this seems to have been canceled at the last minute, literally crossed off the program.[43] In his *New York Times* article announcing the tour, John Martin lists Limón's *The Exiles* among the dances to be performed on the tour; however, *The Exiles*, considered to be one of Limón's masterpieces, does not appear on any of the programs from the tour.[44]

It is well known that, in his dances, Limón strove to create, "works that are involved with man's basic tragedy and the grandeur of his spirit."[45] Limón often used narrative structures, based on literary or biblical themes, to explore the characters of his heroes and heroines and the motivations for their actions. In *La Malinche*, based on the Mexican legend of a peasant girl who became the mistress of Cortez, but later betrayed him to lead her people in a revolution against the Spanish Conquistadors, Limón used a trio consisting of El Conquistador, La Malinche, and El Indio (her peasant lover) to explore themes of love, politics, and betrayal. Limón chose the tragic tale of Othello for his masterpiece, signature work, *The Moor's Pavane*, with music by Henry Purcell. The dance explores the relationships between characters as Limón unfolded this drama of possessive love, deceit, betrayal, and murder within the formal patterns of a recurring court dance. Limón based *The Visitation* on the biblical story of the Annunciation, which was first told to him by his grandmother during his early childhood in Mexico. Of his inspiration for this dance, he wrote,

> "there was the strange, and to a child almost unbearably beautiful story of the simple Jewish girl named Mary, and her exalted destiny, which became *The Visitation*."[46]

The program note from the dance's premiere performance in 1952 indicates the tone of the piece:

> "This dance is based on the legend of the Annunciation, in which the lives of two lowly human beings were transfigured utterly by a celestial messenger. It tells of omnipotence and the great mystery of faith."[47]

The dances of Doris Humphrey expressed similar humanist concerns. *Ritmo Jondo* [Deep Rhythm] portrays Humphrey's vision of the relationships between men and women within Basque culture, a dance "'of men, of women, of meeting and parting.'"[48] John Martin called it, "'a superbly moody and high mettled drama in abstraction.'"[49] *Day on Earth* presents a philosophical look at a man who confronts his relationships with the three women in his life: his first love, his wife, and his daughter; he is finally left all alone and finds solace in his work. *Variations and Conclusions from New Dance* depicts Humphrey's view of a Utopian society, "'the world as it could and should be: a modern brotherhood of man.'"[50] Her humorous *Story of Mankind* presents a satirical look at man and womankind through the ages. *Night Spell* explores the theme of dreams and nightmares, with Limón depicting the dreamer. Humphrey's *Ruins and Visions*, based on Stephen Spender's poem *The Fates*, presents themes of war, insensitivity, and the redemption of humankind through brotherhood in a series of dramatic vignettes.

Both Humphrey and Limón explored the human condition through their dances. The greed and materialism that Americans had come to represent in the world was not found in their works. In fact, both Humphrey and Limón cared little for money over and above what they needed to survive and to keep creating and performing new works. The dances they presented on the tour gave a view of Americans concerned with the plight of mankind, not wealth and material goods.[51] This was exactly the image that the U.S. government needed to present in South America to make their economic policies appear less self-interested.

One of the dances that was not taken on the tour was Limón's *The Traitor*. The piece premiered in August of 1954 and elicited a rave review from *The New York Herald Tribune's* dance critic, Walter Terry. It explored the theme of betrayal and was based on the story of Judas Iscariot and The Last Supper, but it was inspired by the Rosenberg trial. Limón describes the genesis of this dance:

> *The Traitor* was the result of my horror at the execution of two Americans, husband and wife, in peacetime, for treason and espionage against their country; and the spectacle of Russians who, in turn, abandoned their country and defected to the West.[52]

The dance was choreographed for a cast of eight men, which would have made it an impractical choice to bring on the tour.[53] The content of the piece, however, may also have been seen as embarrassing to the U.S. at a time when loyalty was a particularly sensitive issue in light of the Rosenberg trial and the hearings of the House Committee on Un-American Activities.

The Limón company performances were enthusiastically received. Limón described the opening night response at the Teatro Municipal in Rio in a letter to Doris Humphrey.

> It was a triumph ... a brilliant audience – sophisticated, elegant – a magnificent stage – good lights, good orchestra ... The response [to *New Dance*] was enthusiastic and long.
>
> Backstage came the most impressive collection of flowers, and people from the American embassy (who were very pleased and proud and relieved – as one of them said, "We knew this was supposed to be good, but we didn't know it was also polished.") and Brazilians, Argentines and other elegant and distinguished foreigners – much photographing of me with big-wigs from the embassy and the arts – quite fabulous – and very successful ... So you can see that it was in the nature of a notable event – and we can, I think, chalk up a considerable triumph for the American dance.[54]

Limón wrote Humphrey from Montevideo to report that the audiences in São Paulo had been small but enthusiastic, and that the Montevideo performances were also well-received. Alvin Schulman described a touching tribute from the orchestra in Rio.[55] John Martin reported that the company performed to sold-out crowds at all their tour stops and received many invitations to return to South America.[56] Public Affairs Officer John Vebber commended the company's success in his official report to the USIA.

All critics ranged from favorable to highly favorable in their reviews. Of particular note is the fact that one writer not usually friendly to the U.S. also had high praise for this dance group. Audiences were enthusiastic....Throughout their stay in Rio, José Limón and company were most cooperative and made a very favorable impression on the many persons with whom they came in contact.[57]

Some of the pieces presented were received more enthusiastically than others. Schulman reported that *New Dance* and *The Moor's Pavane* were the most popular; *Story of Mankind, La Malinche, The Visitation, Ritmo Jondo,* and *Ruins and Visions* were less so. Martin states that the *Vivaldi Concerto Grosso* was the favorite of South American audiences while *Night Spell* and *Variations and Conclusions* were also extremely popular. He lists *Day on Earth* and *Story of Mankind* as being less well-received.[58]

That the 1954 tour was organized to help further the United States' political agenda in Latin America is clear. How much influence the Limón company performances had on the outcome of the Rio Economic Conference is difficult, if not impossible to determine. John Martin deemed the tour a huge diplomatic and artistic success although he did question the ethics of using art for political purposes.[59] The American delegation to the Rio Economic Conference also considered the conference successful. The delegation held to their stated positions and did manage to persuade the South Americans that these were adequately generous to Latin America. There was some tension, however, as mentioned earlier, especially on the issues of price supports for Latin American commodities and raw materials, and on the U.S. refusal to finance the Inter-American bank.[60]

It is ironic that Limón's work was used to counter the prevailing image of Americans as greedy and materialistic. The economic policy positions presented by the U.S. at the Rio Conference fell short of the requests made by the South American nations on several key points. In fact, the economic policies presented were carefully tailored to protect U.S. economic interests and those of private foreign investors. Concerted diplomatic efforts were made by the American delegation to persuade South American officials to acquiesce to the U.S. positions. The performances of the Limón company in Rio at the time of the conference undoubtedly helped in this persuasion.

The State Department arranged four more tours of the Limón company to politically sensitive areas over the next eighteen years. In 1957, the Limón company toured Europe; their performances in Eastern Europe were of particular diplomatic value. In 1960, the company made a more extensive tour of Latin America. In 1963, the company made a four-month tour to Southeast Asia. The final tour, to the Soviet Union, occurred in January of 1973, one month after Limón's death.

The relationship between the arts (particularly dance) and American politics and foreign relations is often overlooked; however, during the height of the Cold War, many government officials and politicians considered the arts to be a valuable weapon in the fight against Communism. The perceived need to provide artists for the export of American culture fueled the drive toward the formation of the National Endowment for the Arts in 1965. As Representative Frank Thompson commented, "if we are going to use the arts increasingly in our foreign policy we are soon going to have to do something to encourage the arts to grow here at home or we won't have anything at all to export."[61] With the fall of the USSR in 1991, the Cold War officially ended, although some historians became aware of the Soviet Union's imminent demise in 1989.[62] Curiously, 1989 is also the year that the NEA came under sharp attacks from the religious right which crippled, and nearly killed, federal funding of the arts in America. At this time, when federal funding for the arts is scarce, it may prove useful to examine those artists who have been supported in the past, the content of work that has been funded, and the benefit (or perceived benefit) reaped for the U.S. government or for the American people. It may also help artists to understand or examine the political implications for the use of their work and thereby make decisions that are consonant with their personal ethics and values.

Notes

1. Naima Prevots, "$410 – Was That a Necessary Expense?" *Society of Dance History Scholars (U.S.) Conference (15th: 1992: University of California, Riverside): American Dance Abroad,* 2.
2. John Martin, "The Dance: A Tour: Limón to South America with Government Aid," *The New York Times* (14 November 1954).
3. Alvin Schulman, "The Modern Dance Goes to South America," *Dance Observer* (March 1955), 33.
4. Letter from Robert Schnitzer, International Exchange Program, to Julius Bloom, 28 October 1954, collection of the José Limón Dance Foundation, New York.
5. Griffin Fariello, *Red Scare: Memories of the Inquisition: An Oral History* (New York: W W Norton & Company, 1995), 177–180.
6. Stephen J. Whitfield, *The Culture of the Cold War* (Baltimore: Johns Hopkins University, 1991, rev. 1996), 32.
7. Godfrey Hodgson, *America in Our Time* (Garden City, NY: Doubleday, 1976), 40.
8. From a State Department directive, quoted in Whitfield, 39.
9. Laurence Urdang, ed., *The Timetables of American History* (New York: Simon and Schuster, 1981), 360.
10. Urdang, 362.
11. Whitfield, 89.
12. Urdang, 362.
13. Whitfield, 21, 23.
14. "Meeting of Ministers of Finance or Economy of the American Republics as the Fourth Extraordinary Meeting of the Inter-American Economic and Social Council (Rio Economic Conference), Held at Quitandinha, Brazil, November 22– December 2, 1954."

Foreign Relations of the United States 1952–1954 Vol. IV: The American Republics (Washington: US Govt. Printing Office, 1983), 324.

15. From minutes of a meeting of FOA personnel held 24 June 1954. "Meeting of the Ministers of Finance or Economy of the American Republics," *Foreign Relations of the United States 1952–1954 Vol. IV* (Washington: US Govt. Printing Office, 1983), 321.

16. Ibid., 322; confidential memorandum from Assistant Secretary of State for Inter-American Affairs, Holland, to Under Secretary of State, Smith, 1 September 1954, "Meeting of Ministers of Finance or Economy of the American Republics," *Foreign Relations of the United States 1952–1954 Vol. IV: The American Republics* (Washington: US Govt. Printing Office, 1983) 322, 330–331.

17. "Meeting of the Ministers of Finance or Economy of the American Republics," *Foreign Relations of the United States 1952–1954 Vol. IV* (Washington: US Govt. Printing Office, 1983), 321, 323–326, 328, 331, 333–340, 342, 346, 349–351, 353–354.

18. Ibid., 335–338.

19. The first entry pertaining to the South American tour appears on 14 October 1954 in Limón's appointment book. Pages dated October 10–13 are missing. His diary contains an entry pertaining to details of the tour on October 18, the day before his meeting with Schnitzer. José Limón, Appointment Book, Diary. José Limón, Papers. Dance Collection, New York Public Library for the Performing Arts.

20. Robert Schnitzer to Julius Bloom, 28 October 1954, collection of the José Limón Dance Foundation, New York.

21. José Limón, Diary. José Limón, Papers. Dance Collection, New York Public Library.

22. Limón Diary, 29 October 1954.

23. E. W. Kenworthy, "Whitney Trust Got Aid," *The New York Times* (25 February 1967), p. 1, col. 5, p. 10, col. 4–6.

24. Thomas W. Braden, "I'm Glad the CIA is Immoral," *Saturday Evening Post* (20 May 1967), 12.

25. Eva Cockcroft, "Abstract Expressionism: Weapon of the Cold War," *Artforum* xii, no. 10 (June 1974).

26. Ibid.

27. Ibid., 40.

28. Isaac Stern, "Cultural Mission to Iceland," *The New York Times* (23 January 1955).

29. John Martin, "The Dance: A Major Force Enters the Field," *The New York Times* (12 January 1947).

30. Modern dancer and choreographer Merce Cunningham began his collaboration with avant-garde composer John Cage in the mid-1940s. He created *Sixteen Dances for Soloist and Company of Three*, the first of his dances to use indeterminacy as a choreographic device, in 1951. He continued to work with structures based on indeterminacy choreographing *Untitled Solo*, *Dime a Dance*, and *Suite by Chance* in 1953. In her review of a 1953 modern dance concert at which *Sixteen Dances* was performed, Doris Hering wrote that Cunningham, "'seemed like a creature from another planet.'" In 1955, the ANTA dance panel debated whether or not to approve Cunningham for an International Exchange Program tour. John Cage had already been approved by the music panel. According to Naima Prevots, the panel ultimately decided against sending Merce Cunningham as a representative of American culture on the grounds that, "Cunningham was 'confusing and abstract' and that he was not representative of American dance.'" Moira Roth, "The Aesthetic of Indifference," *Artforum*, xvi, no. 3 (November 1997), 46; Roger Copeland, "Beyond Expressionism: Merce Cunningham's Critique of 'the Natural,'" in *Dance History: An Introduction*, ed. by Janet Adshead-Lansdale and June Layson (London: Routledge, 1983, 1994), 189–190; Susan Au, *Ballet and Modern Dance* (London: Thames and Hudson, 1988), 155; Doris Hering quoted in Copeland, 190; Prevots, 6.

31. Martin, "The Dance: A Tour: Limón to South America with Government Aid," *The New York Times* (14 November 1954).

32. Sally Hope to José Limón, 6 December 1954, Montevideo, Uruguay. Pauline Lawrence Limón Collection. Folder 15–16. Dance Collection, New York Public Library.

33. José Limón to Doris Humphrey, 10 December 1954, Montevideo, Uruguay. Doris Humphrey Collection. Microfilm, reel 11. Dance Collection, New York Public Library.

34. John M. Vebber, Public Affairs Officer, United States Information Service, Rio de Janeiro to United States Information Service, Washington, DC, 9 December 1954. Collection of the José Limón Dance Foundation.

35. Letter from José Limón to Doris Humphrey. 24 November 1954. Rio de Janeiro. Humphrey Collection. Microfilm, reel 11. Dance Collection, New York Public Lib

36. Alvin Schulman, "The Modern Dance Goes to South America," *Dance Observer* (N 1955), 33.

37. Percy Warner to U.S. State Department. 10 October, 1960. Porto Alegre, Brazil. J. Limón, papers. Microfilm, reel 9. Dance collection, New York Public Library.

38. Barbara Pollack, "José Limón & Co. in Europe," *Dance Magazine* (April 1958), 77–78.

39. "DC Representative Presents Capenio Award to Limón," *Dance News* (April 1964), 5.

40. José Limón, unpublished autobiography. Dance Collection, New York Public Library.

41. Schulman, 33.

42. Martin, "The Dance: A Tour," (14 November 1954).

43. Based on examination of the programs from the tour in José Limón Papers, 1954–1958. Dance Collection, New York Public Library.

44. Ibid., Martin, "The Dance: A Tour," (14 November 1954).

45. José Limón, "José Limón: An American Accent," *The Modern Dance: Seven Statements of Belief*, ed. Selma Jeanne Cohen (Middletown, CT: Wesleyan University, 1965), 23.

46. José Limón quoted in Martha Hill's "José Limón and his Biblical Works," *Choreography and Dance* v. 2, pt. 3 (1992), 59.

47. Ibid., 59.

48. Doris Humphrey quoted in Selma Jeanne Cohen's *Doris Humphrey: An Artist First* (Middletown, CT: Wesleyan University Press, 1972), 204.

49. Quoted in Cohen's *Doris Humphrey*, 205.

50. Doris Humphrey quoted in Marcia Siegel's *Days on Earth: The Dance of Doris Humphrey* (New Haven: Yale University Press, 1987), 157.

51. This was the case with many American modern dancers and choreographers. Martha Graham explored what she called, "deep matters of the heart" in her works. Her company was sent on an ANTA sponsored tour to Asia in 1956, and to the Middle East and Eastern Europe in 1962. Helen Tamiris's dances often explored themes of racism and social injustice. However, the political content of her work and her involvement with Marxist causes in the 1930s could possibly have removed her from consideration by the ANTA dance panel. Katherine Dunham made several foreign tours, none with government support. Her 1951 performance in Santiago, Chile of *Southland*, which depicted a lynching, proved to be too strong fare for State Department officials. The State Department repressed performances of *Southland*, and consistently denied government support and sponsorship for the company's foreign tours. ANTA sent the Alvin Ailey Dance Company on a tour of Southeast Asia in 1962. ANTA also supported the foreign tours of several major American ballet companies including New York City Ballet, American Ballet Theatre, the Joffrey Ballet, and San Francisco Ballet. This was presumably to counter the influence of the Russian exportation of ballet to the West. Martha Graham, *A Dancers' World*, 1957, film; Arthur Todd, "Dance as United States Cultural Ambassador," *Impulse* (1963–1964), 33–43; Constance Valis Hill, "Katherine Dunham's *Southland*: Protest in the Face of Repression," *Dance Research Journal* v. 26, no. 2 (Fall 1994), 1–10; Stacey Prickett, "'The People': Issues of Identity within the Revolutionary Dance," *Of, By and For the People: Dancing on the Left in the 1930s*, ed. Lynn Garafola, *Studies in Dance History*, vol. 5, no. 1 (Spring 1994), 20.

52. Limón, *The Modern Dance: Seven Statements of Belief*, 26.

53. Barbara Pollack and Charles Humphrey Woodford, *Dance is a Moment: A Portrait of José Limón in Words and Pictures* (Pennington, NJ: Princeton Book Company, Publishers, 1993), 38.

54. José Limón to Doris Humphrey, 24 November 1954. Doris Humphrey Collection. Microfilm, reel 11. Dance Collection, New York Public Library.

55. Schulman, 33.
56. Martin, "The Dance: Diplomacy: Limón Makes Conquest in South America," *The New York Times* (23 January 1955).
57. John Vebber to USIA, Rio de Janeiro, 9 December 1954. Collection of José Limón Dance Foundation.
58. Martin, "The Dance: Diplomacy," *The New York Times* (23 January 1955).
59. Ibid.
60. "Meeting of Ministers of Finance or Economy of the American Republics," *Foreign Relations of the United States*.
61. Representative Frank Thompson (D-NJ) quoted in Cary Larson's The Reluctant Patron: The United States Government and the Arts, 1943–1965 (Philadelphia: University of Pennsylvania Press, 1983), 118.
62. Reinhold Wagnleitner, *Coca-Colonization and the Cold War: The Cultural Mission of the United States in Austria After the Second World War*, trans. Diana M. Wolf (Chapel Hill, NC: University of North Carolina Press, 1994), 1.

12

THE ESSENCE OF HUMANITY:
JOSÉ LIMÓN AFTER A HALF CENTURY

Sarah Stackhouse

As a dancer, José was passionate, spontaneous, and Dionysian. On stage, in his dramatic works, he displayed powerful impulse, attack and thrust. Being face to face with him or being lifted by him could be overwhelming. His movement was huge and consumed all of the space around him. He would send his body into the air by sheer will and determination or plunge to the floor with little care for his own safety. He seemed to push the space; to pull it after him, to crash through it. He didn't cater to neatness. Proper placement or prettiness in dancing were never considerations for him. "When you stop trying to be pretty", he said to his students, "you will be beautiful". If he asked for a balance, it was in order to have a moment's suspension from which to fall or to dart out into space. When he wanted line and form in his dances, it was for the purpose of guiding the viewer's eye into the human dimension.

As a choreographer and in the consummate forming of his works we see the contemplator, the classicist. Limón's choreography embodies the impulse and drive of his dancing, but it is clear that the Apollonian mind was there informing his thought and giving shape to his creation. He had great skill in developing and varying movement from a supreme economy of thematic material. His works based on theme and variation are so harmoniously conceived that it is hard to imagine any gesture, motion or choreographic element not being essential to the whole. Arching melodious phrases of movement and masterful counterpoint flowed from him, adding dimension to the music. Few other choreographers of this century have succeeded in interweaving sound and motion in such a rich and eloquent texture.

In my first class with José at the American Dance Festival (ADF) at Connecticut College in 1954, after being overwhelmed by performances of *The Visitation*, now tragically lost, and *The Traitor*, I knew in my blood and bones that I must dance in his company. After graduation from the University of Wisconsin dance program, I studied in N.Y. in José's repertory class in the morning and often played hooky from my evening work to attend his technique class. I joined an augmented company for *Missa*

Brevis the following summer with performances at ADF then again the next year for a United States Information Agency/State Department tour of South America in 1960. After that tour José asked me to be in his permanent company. During the next three years of US touring, I had small parts in *There is a Time* and *I, Odysseus* and was responsible for costume care. With little performing to do I would sit in the wings every night to study and bask in the glow of the artistry of Limón, Lucas Hoving, Betty Jones, Ruth Currier and Pauline Koner.

Before long José asked me to be demonstrator/assistant in his classes and to teach at Juilliard, and at ADF where the company was in residence for 6 weeks each summer. It was utter joy to be in José's repertory and technique classes day after day and to be present as he spun out choreography for the students. Opportunities to study with him "downtown" were few so it was a rare chance to continue to be exposed daily to his dancing power and beauty. His awesome, fearless, impulsive attack, the feeling that movement came spontaneously from him as though unstudied, technique submerged in purpose, his utter economy of movement, his hunger for and his impassioned consuming of space, were the guides he offered his students by example. He spoke of breath and weight and suspension and what he did in movement was the truth of it. I have since studied and danced with other artists and find that, no matter what the material, those are the essentials of compelling dancing.

Limón spoke often in his classes and rehearsals of the "Dionysian" and the "Apollonian." He emphasized the Dionysian because it was decidedly the stuff of his dancing. But he wanted to see both qualities in his dancers and in his dances. He often based the tension in his works on the struggle between them and he wanted that struggle to show. In *The Traitor* Limón's substance and weight as the contemptible "Traitor"/Judas is in stark contrast to Lucas Hoving's levitating, floating "Leader"/Christ figure. In *The Emperor Jones*, Limón's driving madness as "Jones" contrasts with the cool calculating "White Man" of Hoving; in *Missa Brevis* Limón's lone, questioning figure is in contrast to the strong unity and surety of the group. Walter Terry in a review of Limón's *Chaconne* described that solo as "... aristocratic in form and treatment, yet charged with primitive strength and pride."[1] This contrasting theme of the Apollonian and the Dionysian runs throughout Limón's choreography in different proportions in different works and describes much of the foundation of his artistry as dancer and as maker of dances. Now as I stage and direct his dances for companies around the world as well as for the Limón Company, the challenge is to investigate how these qualities can be brought out in dancers of a different time and training.

The duality of peasant/aristocrat is another fecund preoccupation of Limón in his choice of subject matter, his way of working, and his

Louis Falco and Sarah Stackhouse in *A Choreographic Offering*. Photo by Fannie Meltzer.

aesthetic. His natural bearing was invariably aristocratic, elevated. His interactions with his dancers were generous but usually quite formal. He was seldom critical and never harsh in his direction. He came from well-educated parents of some status in Mexico. The family had Spanish ancestry as well as some unspoken of Yaqui Indian blood. His father was a musician; his mother a housewife. When the family immigrated to the US his father had to struggle for a bare subsistence. In addition to this dramatic shift of fortune, José suffered the indignities of prejudice as a young Mexican boy in this country. It is clear from his soon to be published autobiographical writings that he thought of himself as an outsider and identified with the minority, the underclass and working people. When I first encountered Limón at Connecticut College in the summer of 1954 I remember seeing him sitting and talking almost daily with the workers as they had lunch in the shade outside the studio where he had just given class. His reverence for the peasant, the respect for his Indian heritage and his desire to ascribe to the peasant the same dignity as that given to the aristocrat is embodied in the powerfully dynamic male solos of *The Unsung*. "It [*The Unsung*] reeks with male sweat, suffering, silence and pride…"[2]

My most profound experience as a dancer with José, the choreographer, was during the 1964 creation of his particularly Apollonian work, *A Choreographic Offering*. This piece was in homage to Doris Humphrey, his teacher, mentor and the artistic director of his company for many years. Movement motifs and phrases from the body of her work gave him the thematic material, which he re-ignited with his own genius and artistry, creating a new and homogeneous context. In addition, this choreography was in honor of J.S. Bach and the *Musical Offering*, which he loved passionately. For at least a year before he began to create with the dancers, during the 3 month 1963 Asian tour, he was listening to the music daily. Whenever we weren't traveling, he was in the theater with *Musical Offering* reverberating through the empty spaces, his Wollensak tape recorder at his side, playing the music. At the end of the tape he would rewind it and begin it anew. He was ingesting the music, swimming in it. He did his warm up to it; put on his makeup to it. Sometimes I would see him sitting with his eyes closed letting the beauty of the music wash over him. He had every note in his fiber long before he began work with us on his choreographic offering.

Finally, the lush round movement phrases and elegant forms began to flow out of him, it seemed spontaneously. Gradually we would feel the music coming into new form as the choreography expanded in its dimensions. Sometimes he would begin rehearsal by saying "The demons of choreography kept me awake all night. Let's start over children." He would discard a nearly complete section of what we thought was marvelous contrapuntal and layered group choreography, then begin again and have a new section by the end of our 3-hour rehearsal period. One evening Alice Condodina, one of the original cast, joked with him. "I'm going to make a dance out of all the material you throw out." José responded, "Of course, my dear, it's yours!"

Along, with the *Chaconne*, *The Moor's Pavane*, and *Concerto Grosso*, *A Choreographic Offering* is an example of Limón's rich Apollonian classicism. Of the *Offering* Arma Kisselgoff wrote that "[Limón] used form at its most abstract to distill emotions with depth and clarity."[3] In the *Offering*, the movement material and the spatial forms are the subject matter. He focused on them with eloquent and detailed choreographic treatment. When working in a dramatic or romantic vein, Limón often used movement, timing, phrasing, or inflection contributed by his soloists. But in the *Offering* his use of Humphrey's movement material and his choreography were very specific. He delineated the contours of the phrasing and the relation to the music, the formality of the space, and the design and shape of the movement. Anyone familiar with Humphrey's dances will identify her material easily. At the same time the viewer will recognize and be drawn into the mind and vision of the very different artistic temperament of José Limón.

In *A Choreographic Offering*, the spirit is exuberant, full of humanity, hope and optimism in the suspensions; daring in the swoops and, under curves; thrilling in its lively tempo and call for virtuosity. The movement looks spontaneous, effusive and uncluttered. He accomplished a multi-layered simplicity through his profound musicality, skill with counterpoint and his fully dimensional forms. There's a strong sense of the folkloric, often found in both Humphrey's and Limón's work, in the rhythmic drive and patterning and in the spatial designs with dancers linked together, hand to hand in lines twisting through various contours; in circles with repeated step figures; and in unison movement which draws the dancers into a harmonious unit. Again, the noble peasant.

In works with a dramatic theme, such as *The Moor's Pavane*, José used a dynamic line with strong contrasts in energy and in flow. A characteristic high energy attack, for example, may oppose a lighter flow of movement or a bound and restricted texture contrast the large free flow of a swing. In the *Offering* however, the energy and flow contrasts are subtle and more attention is drawn to the spatial dynamic. He kept the spatial contrasts pulsing and vibrating throughout; from a solo in which the dancer shapes and decorates the space, to a tight, parallel unison of a duet, to a quintet which swirls the space and sends it flying, to the large adagio ensemble in which the dancers become the space, flowing and changing in sumptuous forms. The rich melodic shaping of the movement phrases soars with optimism in this euphoric work.

The *Offering* is replete with Limón's stunning mastery of transition as well. The sections flow, one brought on by another with seamless beauty. After the opening (*Dance with 9*) the group finishes center, then walks away in silence, revealing a female solo figure. She begins four short solos. On the last solo, an adagio, four men enter, lift her to walk on air then hover in the ether. They set her down and lead her in canons earthward. Finally the men make a pathway of their backs on which she walks, levitating in silence and disappears into the wings. From the other side of the stage, with new music, five whirlers enter sending the air spinning. They establish a new pathway for another female soloist to come leaping by and fly into a virtuosic allegro dance as the five exit. Thus Limón weaves the choreographic thread, giving continuity and rich texture in the layering and three dimensionality of his work.

In creating transitions there were no capricious blackouts for José. When he did use a blackout it was well chosen to give a breath, a moment's rest for the eye, or in order to bring the light up again on a dramatically striking contrast. One of the most stunning examples of such a moment occurs after the adagio ensemble of 22 dancers has filled the space with horizontal flow for 6 minutes. Black out, dancers clear, then a center pool of light comes up on a lone female figure poised on one leg, arms overhead and torso arched to the side toward the lifted leg. She seems to be suspended in vertical space. What a beautilul moment! He focuses on the present by framing it in what has just passed.

Limón's use of exits and entrances was extremely economical as well. In sectional dances such as *There is a Time* and *A Choreographic Offering*, he introduced a subject and then followed it through on stage generally without comings and goings. In the *Finale* of the *Offering* however, he used the device of entrances and exits to create a continuous flow of movement from upstage left to downstage right. Again and again the dancers come and go reiterating the lushness of Humphrey's phrases in Limón's passionate and soaring context. In addition, the density of space modulates throughout this section to heighten the effect. It begins with a weighted solo, which marks the space; small groups enter and swirl around; the soloist exits; the groups exit as a duet enters and stretches the diagonal; a large mass coalesces to lift a figure high. More solos, duets and groups of increasing size go by until all the dancers are together in what seems the inexorable flow of humanity in a great river of time. This pulsing and amplification of the spatial dynamic along with a unidirectional progress of entrances and exits creates a powerful emotional impact. Throughout the *Offering*, the spirit is lifted by José's humanism; exalted with his majestic classicism.

José said once that he wasn't a choreographer. Why he felt that I do not know, but he most certainly was in his deepest core a choreographer. He needed to choreograph. He loved it and thrived on it. Classes with him were marvels of theme and variation. He couldn't stop. Often, when he returned a retired dance to the repertory he would re-choreograph parts of it. He wasn't interested in faithful "restorations". He didn't like to fuss with the past. His thought and interest, his artistry were always moving on. Moreover, because his creative methods were so linked to the particular dancers with whom he was working, a change in cast seemed to stimulate his creativity. New artistry ... new ideas. When Pauline Koner left the company he made a new *Time to Laugh* solo (from *There is a Time*). She had supplied some of the original material and it was just right for her lively accented and rhythmic quality. When I was given the role my longer limbs and different training didn't do justice to that movement so he choreographed a new and just as wonderful romp; more spatial and sweeping; less ornate and decorative. Both were marvelous expressions of laughter.

He kept creating in the natural process of artistic evolution, often besting himself with subsequent versions. The earliest work film of José dancing his solo *Chaconne* premiered in 1942 shows very complicated and convoluted movement sequences which seem to me unrelated to the space. For me, it lacked a center of gravity. Much of it had been created in his small apartment. The next film made in 1954, again with José dancing, is somewhat simplified and clearer. Then in the mid 60's he taught the material to a repertory class, refining the choreographic line to such a point that the rich variation and texture could truly emerge enhanced by a new open and swirling spatial logic. Very important in this last version I think, was that he was no longer the dancer and could now stand apart and see the dance with the broad view of the choreographer's eye.

José's *The Exiles*, a dance based on Adam and Eve's expulsion from the Garden of Eden, underwent 3 transformations with different casts. The original was made for Letitia Ide and himself in 1947. I didn't see this version and there is sadly no film of it. From photographs and accounts of this duet, I sense that the next incarnation of *The Exiles* with Ruth Currier in the female role was very different. Both José's and Letitia's physical forms were Michelangelesque. Ruth, on the other hand, was the embodiment of Bosch's fragile Eve, delicate and vulnerable next to José's solid mass. It seems to me, in studying the film of Ruth and José dancing, that much of Ruth's movement was quite personal to her and was probably contributed by her. José undoubtedly recreated much of the choreography for the two of them, finding a new expression in the different balance of their frames alone and together.

The work took on a new form yet again when José revived it for Louis Falco and me. The dance was reshaped to fit our bodies and make use of our characteristics. Here too, José could stand apart and gain the choreographer's distance and perspective. I think that his artistic evolution had brought him in this period (1965) to a much broader use of space and a stronger integration of movement and space in general. This third version of *The Exiles* used a more rangy and voluminous sense of space with less intricate movement. Although he seldom spoke to us of his point of view, I sense from photos and film that in the previous versions José had seen Adam and Eve as Man and Woman whereas he was seeing us as very young creatures, barely formed and just beginning to discover our existence.

Over the years one sees his works growing from small chamber pieces, gradually expanding to the rich layering of voices in slightly larger works like *The Traitor*, to the orchestration in others such as *Missa Brevis*. The works get larger in numbers of dancers and push out the perimeters of the space. José was always on the edge financially. He never had his own studio, but Martha Hill, Director of the Juilliard Dance Department, gave him rehearsal space in the evenings. He also had the use of many talented student dancers on whom he developed material and created the large sections for some of his works. In addition he had received funding from the State Department to support a larger group of dancers for the tours of South America and the Far East.

After the 1963 USIA Asian tour many of the dancers who had been with him in his formative works moved on for various reasons and José had a new company made up of mostly Juilliard graduates. They were a different generation, with different background and study. Style, technique and temperaments were different. His first work with this group was the *Offering* followed in 1966 by *The Winged* which used the theme of creatures of flight – real, imagined and mythological. In it he used the metaphor of winged creatures to investigate and highlight the salient features and strengths of these dancers in very personal works. There was Louis Falco as the untamed "Pegasus", Jennifer Muller as the voluptuous and virtuosic "Sphinx", Betty Jones as a very "Rara Avis" and many others. After having worked so intensely with Humphrey's material in the classical framework of the *Offering*, he strode out in *The Winged* with radically different movement configurations. The piece is physically demanding and effusive in style. Here he explored and exploited a wide dynamic and spatial range and based the timing and phrasing on the breath. Always a master of chamber work, José mixed thrilling solos, intimate duets, and small groups with big, sweeping masses of figures.

He wanted silence to surround these creatures of flight. He used some ambient music and nature sounds, but much of the dance basked in silence. He let the dance breathe on its own without the domination of metered accompaniment. In the silences one could sense the sound of the air around the movement; the modulation of foot sounds on the floor, from soft padding sounds to sharp percussive ones; small sounds of cupped hands beating together or the implied sound of air moving through wings. It's stirring to "hear" the movement. He poured forth his passion for the human mind and body free to soar in an elastic framework of silence, to live out a phrase, or to compact it according the breath of life of the moment. It was the elegant silence and sparse score surrounding the dancers along with the stunning personal portraits that gave *The Winged* its great beauty. This marvelous work was revived at Juilliard by Carla Maxwell in 1996 with a new score commissioned through the efforts of Benjamin Harkarvy by The Juilliard School and composed by Jon Magnussen. It has recently been given glorious performances with live music as part of the 50th anniversary of the founding of the Limón Company at the Riverside Church in New York City.

José made two other works without musical score in his last years: *The Unsung* and *Carlota*. He liked to work solely from his own aesthetic, in part perhaps because he had had some very unsatisfactory scores written for his works in the late '60's. *The Unsung* is based on legendary American Indian figures although the movement is abstract. A group of eight men creates a rhythmic network out of which emerge remarkable, physically demanding solos for each man. The dancers use strong percussive sounds with the feet; dynamic thrust and attack seem to yell out in anger or pain; elevations that come from nowhere crash to the floor. All of the body's angles punctuate these dances. The silence allows us to hear every effort, every exhausted breath with unique dramatic effect in this virile dance. Again José developed a new, compelling and evocative movement language that is stunning in its invention, abstract yet gripping in its impact. His last work *Carlota*, is based on the life of the wife of Maximillian, short-lived Emperor of Mexico. José used the story line format but the work has an abstract quality even as it is being descriptive. Limón's artistry with movement and rhythm is again proven in this stark, austere expression.

With full houses, curtain call after curtain call, thrilling dancing, enthusiastic reviews, the recently completed 50th anniversary season has shown that the works of José Limón are speaking today with great relevance and modernity. The Limón Company is thriving and vibrant 25 years after José's death, thanks in great part to the undaunted spirit, vision and resiliency of Carla Maxwell, the Artistic Director. It is a new time with a new generation of dancers. Few of the present company saw or knew José. Though they never studied with him, they have learned the thrust, impulse and daring of his movement; they are finding breath and suspension. José's uncluttered, unprettied choreography demands personal clarity, balance and harmony, honesty and maturity. The company has dancers of a wide age range, including those at the very beginning of their careers who foster these qualities and continue to grow with them. They have distinctive characteristics as dancers and are highly disciplined as a group. They accept the assiduous coaching and endless refinement of detail which clarifies the form and brings out the expression of Limón's works. They relish the humanism of these works and they are willing to be present and revealed in them. The mind and senses of these artists resonate with Limón's choreography. It tells me that we are coming out of the time in which expression and humanism were suspect. Innovation and virtuosity in movement and choreography for effect alone are beginning to wear thin. José's work is being rediscovered.

As one entrusted to set Limón's works I continue to investigate the multi-layered expression necessary to bring them to fullness of life on stage. In a piece like *The Moor's Pavane*, a quartet based on the legend of Othello, the very personal, idiosyncratic styles of Koner as Emilia and Hoving as Iago, created evocative performances. They contributed detail to José's movement material. It is evident to me that trying to imitate their work would be a mistake and would fail. I have spent hundreds of hours studying the films of the original cast in order to understand José's choreographic intent and structure apart from individual performance and then to see what of those performances is transferable to today's dancers. Once I have a sense of the function of the four roles, their contrasts and how each varies the thematic material, I can guide new dancers in developing and bringing their individual qualities to these roles. Amazingly, each time I return to the films I find new information. I realize again how rich was the illusion created by the movement of the original cast. The illusion moved far beyond the sum of the physical components of the dance and those dancers.

Setting *Pavane* on ballet companies has been a particularly interesting challenge for me in discovering the essence of the movement qualities and textures of each role and learning how to transfer them. Most of the movement concepts that José worked with are quite different from the ways in which ballet dancers work. Although he didn't often verbalize his ideas, they were unique to his dancing and very present in his choreography. José intuitively used resistance, bound flow and strong attacks which sustain the height of the energy reverberating in space to give massive power to his "Moor". His elegant musicality and phrasing and the way he transferred his weight allowed him to stretch out or compress the time and space and create an expression of overwhelming turmoil and grief. In many ballet companies the dancers do not lower the heel to the floor and usually carry their center of weight high in the torso. The learning process is arduous, but when the dancers are excited by new ideas and willing to work with them, the transformation is miraculous to watch. They no longer have to rely on trying to act the part (few dancers have that training) but physically become the role and rely on the beautifully conceived form of the choreography to feed them the expression.

In reviving *Mazurkas* for the company, I studied the silent film of the original cast. I also brought to the surface my deeply ingrained memories of the piece I had watched nightly with most of the original cast during my second year of touring in 1962. By the end of the 6 week tour I could have gone into any of the dances. José choreographed the solos, duets, trio, quartet dances as gifts to each of the dancers who had been with him on the 1957 tour to Europe. The work was also a tribute to the music of Chopin and the Polish people who had received José's work and the company with unqualified warmth. Several phone conversations with Michael Hollander and Harlan ("Harkie") McCallum of the original cast gave me a lively picture of the company's time in Poland. They described a piano concert in Chopin's home, and José's being profoundly moved by the vital spirit of the Poles who were still trying to rebuild their lives 12 years after the end of World War II.

Carla Maxwell and I had spoken often of reviving *Mazurkas*. Resources finally became available for the project in 1989. Again I studied the film over and over again, absorbing the dances, each so expressive and personal to that dancer: Betty's – bright and clear like the ring of crystal; Ruth's – decorating the space and inviting the pianist to dance with her; Harkie's – zesty and boisterous; Michael's – a last fling before leaving the company; Chester Wolenski's – painful with nostalgia and loss. After understanding the relation between the choreography and the original performers, I needed to dance the work in order to fully understand the subtleties, the phrasing, how the rhythmic patterning interlaced with the music and how the space and movement enhanced each other. By the time I began work with the company, I had all the material in my bones. Many of these dances, although tied to an older generation of performers, seemed to fit our dancers easily. They still required a great deal of coaching to integrate space and movement, the liveliness and character of the mazurka rhythms, and the roundness and richness of expression that transcends pretty dancing. The dances fell into place easily with the music. They were so logically and inevitably entwined with the wonderful Chopin score.

I feel it is important to give up any idea of trying to make one of José's dances work in the way it was first performed; to try to imitate the "original" or to do it "right". That would be death to his vision and could not be further from his way of working. Having spent years with him as an assistant in classes and rehearsals and as a dancer, one of my strongest convictions is that José created and recreated his works to breathe and remain fluid. He didn't want museum replicas or perfectly embalmed dances without life and spontaneity for that brief moment that they are on stage. He disliked neatness, precision, academic, overstudied dances and dancing. I think he liked seeing chaos which would resolve itself into some contrasting, beautiful form. Often subsequent companies' settings have tried to organize and neaten up areas that José meant to be dissonant so have lost that sense of relief and resolution that emerges when a consonant form appears.

There are instances in which I have done some mixing of different versions of a dance which seem to do justice to the new context and allow some beautiful material to float back to the surface. Of course my judgment jumps in here. I have to be present as a mind, as memory, experience and recreator in order to even make the first move. I try to take the cues from José. From the films I see what he changed and try to understand why. In considering the two film versions of *The Exiles* for instance, I recognize the choreographic reasons for the changes made by José beyond those of personal artistry and body form. I feel there were spatial incongruities in the version with Ruth. At times the movement phrases became unnecessarily convoluted and block the flow of the dance's kinesthetic and spatial logic. He was the dancer and could not provide the external perspective. The spatial logic of the version with Louis and me is stronger. In reconstructing this dance I feel we need to let it evolve as José would have. Keeping that clarity of the spatial design and recapturing some of the spontaneity of the movement phrases from the previous version enriches the fabric of the whole.

For most of the works we have only the rawest of work films. Some have no sound and some were shot with such poor light that much of the detail is obscured. Most were made before the dances were seasoned and matured, often filmed in spaces so small that there were changes made from the original choreography to accommodate spatial restrictions. Some of the dances such as *The Visitation* (trio with Limón, Hoving and Koner) were not filmed and were thus lost. Some films that existed were old and of poor quality when finally translated on to video. The process of remounting a work from film can be frustrating. Yet I find the process of understanding and bringing new life to these works is one of endless fascination.

One of the early *The Moor's Pavene* films made in a postage stamp space, however, holds some wonderful clues to bringing out spatial tensions. The close-ups and angle shots helped me understand how José had focused the viewer's eye by the placement or subtle movement of the inactive dancer(s) on stage. I was more aware of the way in which he shifted attention by contrary spatial movement, blurring some dancer(s) to bring others into focus. Another boon from the cramped space of filming was, as Lucas Hoving reports, that José made a crucial change in the last scene in order to fit both Koner and Hoving in the frame with himself (Othello) as he pursues Jones (Desdemona) to kill her. Hoving and Koner slowly and symetrically move from upstage to downstage on an inward angle like a trap closing in on the pursued. The previous version had Hoving upstage right and Koner already downstage left in a pose which drained the attention from the climactic moments of the piece. José saw how effective the new framing device was and changed the dance.

"What would José think of my reworking his choreography?" I have to answer myself by saying that he would like seeing the beauty of his works being given the great care and devotion, intelligence and artistry that I have seen in the dancers who have chosen to perform his work. The enthusiasm with which these artists bring his work to the stage and with which his work is now being accepted have allowed him to transcend his time. His work is modern, as vital now as when he conceived it. I think he would not care that it is not presented exactly as it was originally and would see that it is being recreated with a driving force of life itself with the supreme energy, passion, spirit and humanity that he envisioned and with which he endowed his work.

"Humanism is back"[4] begins Anna Kisselgoff's review of the 50th anniversary season at the Joyce Theater. For José and many artists who refused to be pulled into the black hole of disbelief of the 60's, 70's and 80's, humanism never left town. José once said to me when I was feeling dispirited and indulging in "why bother" feelings, "My dear, as long as we have men in the White House like Nixon, we must continue to do our work with passion. As artists we offer humanity a light to defend itself against darkness and ignorance and decadence." It cleared my head and continues to clear my spirit each time I walk into rehearsal to reinforce that vision and power in the profound works of José Limón.

Notes

1. Walter Terry, *New York Herald Tribune*, August 7, 1950.
2. Linda Howe-Beck, *Montreal Gazette*, October 10, 1980.
3. Anna Kisselgoff, *The New York Times*, October 23, 1997.
4. Ibid.

13

REMEMBERING JOSÉ LIMÓN

June Dunbar

José Limón probably was responsible for the path of my career. One never knows about these things but I suspect that if I had not studied with him immediately following my college graduation, my work life might well have taken another road. It was he who entrusted me with my first teaching assignments in the newly created dance department at The Juilliard School and at the midtown Manhattan studio where I was left in charge of the Limón technique classes when he and his company were on tour. He gave me even more responsibility by asking me to take administrative charge of the studio classes. This meant collecting all the students' fees, assigning teachers and accompanists to classes and paying the rent to the studio owner. All of this was an enormous amount of trust to invest in a twenty-three year old and it was the foundation of a close and lasting friendship that survived until his death in 1972.

Most likely it was José who later suggested to Martha Hill, the founding director of the dance division at Juilliard, that I act on her behalf when she was to be away for the better part of two academic years in 1957 and 1958. Martha was to join her husband, Lefty Davies, in Belgium where he was on assignment as director of the American pavilion at the Brussels World's Fair. In her absence the store needed tending and I was asked by Martha to take that job. Later, upon her return from Europe, she asked me to become her associate director, a role I fulfilled for the next ten years. I saw a great deal of José during this entire period; our paths crossed frequently when he came to teach or to rehearse with his company in Juilliard studios.

Late in 1957, during the period when Martha was in Brussels, José and his company returned to New York after a grueling State Department tour to England, France, Poland and Yugoslavia. José was burning with the idea of a dance which had been inspired by his experiences in Poland during that trip. He wished to use advanced students from his Juilliard classes to augment his company and Martha Hill's approval was needed. She was reached in Belgium by phone and endorsed the scheme. We quickly plunged into the work of producing *Missa Brevis* which premiered on April 11, 1958. José's passion to make this dance was relentless. It

reflected his profound need to pay homage to the courage of the Polish
people and to the spirit with which they survived their wartime ordeal.
He was totally obsessed in his desire to have the dance reflect the depth
of his feelings and experiences in Poland. There was a real urgency since
the project had to be inserted into the already existing, very full Juilliard
production schedule and was to be produced in a relatively short time.
Missa Brevis also required extra resources beyond those allotted to most
of the dance productions at Juilliard during that time. It was, therefore,
my task as producer to coordinate the schedules of the dancers with the
chorus of sixteen, the conductor and organist, as well as to oversee the
building of the costumes. In addition, I had to monitor the budget.

Ming Cho Lee was asked by José to design the setting and costumes
for *Missa Brevis*. Ming created a stark and powerful projection of a
bombed out cathedral, following an idea suggested by José.

Missa Brevis, with music by Zoltan Kodaly, was premiered on time and
was an immediate success. The fact that Martha Hill and William
Schuman, the then president of The Juilliard School, responded immediately and positively to José's need to create this work testifies to the support and generosity given to him by this remarkable institution. José the
artist was unstintingly sustained by this team and we are the richer for
their belief in his vision. Throughout the whole process of the creation of
Missa Brevis I felt like a midwife and the experience of being present at
the birth created a life long bond between José and me.

A man of courtly manners, José often appeared to some as stiff and formal, but I knew him to be wickedly funny, extravagantly generous and
outrageously bawdy. He and all the Juilliard dance teachers hated having
to grade students, but it was one of those tasks that had to be done. He
would put it off as long as possible and always asked for my help at
grading time. He would come to my office where, behind closed doors,
we would tackle the job. José never had difficulty remembering the
names, faces and bodies of the talented students. The problem was that
he blurred all the gray, undistinguished, adequate dancers whose names,
faces and bodies he could not recall. Routinely his first suggestion was
that every student be given a C but quickly realized that this would be a
terrible disservice to the really outstanding students to whom he wished
to give the good grades that they deserved. Class lists in hand, I would
try to jog his memory with physical descriptions such as "tall, straight-
haired, blond" or "very thin with long, narrow feet" or "flexible and
slightly sway-backed". These descriptions seemed inadequate to José
since he wanted to be reminded of the quality of the dancer, not simply
their physical attributes. So we developed a game and established a
ritual at grade-giving time. It employed José's own thoughts about a
dancer's body being like an orchestra, except that in this instance he

asked me to describe *which instrument* in an orchestra a particular dancer looked like or moved like. Silly as this sounds, the device seemed to recall for him a particular dancer and hopefully he would come up with an appropriate grade for that semester. Eventually all sections of the orchestra were used to evoke the dimly remembered students. So and so looked like a "cello" or, worse, a "double bass" (*really* broad hipped), and moved like the sound of a morose oboe. Our discussions about these dancing instruments became more and more outlandish and ribald. We would both end up roaring with laughter, carried away by our juvenile humor. Grades did emerge after these lengthy sessions and there was always a sprinkling of C minuses, but no one, as I recall, was flunked. Although the means of arriving at the grades were unorthodox, the ends worked for him and they were fair. He hated to discourage any dancer who tried hard but did not have much hope of future success in the field as a performer.

My husband and I had a small week-end house in Pennsylvania that was about 45 minutes away from José and Pauline's New Jersey farm. As a result we saw them fairly often. We loved going there because they were marvelous hosts. The farm was a unique place to visit. It was beautifully sited, and handsome in its arrangements of buildings that suggested a village of various dwellings, some attached and others free standing. The former milking barn had been turned into a long, narrow kitchen-dining room with an ample fireplace at one end. Three generous steps at the opposite end led up to a large living room which retained its original structure as a hay barn of soaring proportions. The kitchen was distinctly Pauline's domain. Along the south facing wall was a row of windows underneath which were all the necessary appurtenances for preparing meals. Though the four of us would always be together for drinks before dinner, she would never to sit down with us at the dining table during the meal. Hovering over the three of us, Pauline would bustle back and forth between sink and stove to the huge and handsome refectory table that José had built, to mete out one perfect, beautifully presented dish after dish. Though she may not have actually sat down to eat with us, she was very much part of the conversation, punctuating it with caustic, witty and pithy comments.

One chilly evening, we stopped for dinner at the Limóns on the way to our own house for the week-end and José announced that, for a change, he would be the cook instead of Pauline. He wanted to recreate for us a lunch that he had eaten at Georgia O'Keeffe's adobe house in New Mexico. She had invited him to drive out to Abiquiu from Santa Fe where the company was performing. He was flattered to be the guest of this distinguished artist, but was somewhat apprehensive because as a man of enormous appetite he was afraid that O'Keeffe (by now in her late seventies) might serve him little more than a lettuce leaf or a bowl of thin soup. The meal that José prepared started with a roaring fire in the fireplace. When the coals were a glowing orange he flung a two inch think sirloin steak onto them letting it quickly blacken for a few minutes before turning it over to char it on the other side. The accompaniment to this very rare beef was a salad consisting of parsley, chopped scallions with a quarter of a lemon on the side. There might have been a bit of olive oil as well, but I do not remember it. As José said, "A nice surprise from an old lady!" And for us.

José was a gifted and impassioned gardener and planted many varieties of lilacs near the driveway entrance to the farm. He also grew a large variety of azaleas, and, like many gardeners, wanted instant gratification from his efforts. Where they would be visible from the kitchen, he crowded together an abundance of azaleas in an exuberant display of vivid colors. It was almost a retina shattering sight. There were also more subdued plantings of irises and spring flowering daffodils and tulips among other perennials which burst forth in spring. Since many of his summers were spent at Connecticut College, he seemed to concentrate his gardening efforts for their ultimate reward in April and May.

The foundation of a small building which had collapsed during a severe storm not long after the Limóns acquired the property formed the stone walls for a courtyard that José turned into a lovely green oasis. In all his travels he made a habit of bringing back cuttings of evergreen ivy and planting them at the base of the walls of this outdoor room. Before many years this place of retreat was entirely grown up with reminders of green places in the Escorial, Williamsburg, the Piazzale Michelangelo in Florence, Versailles, Connecticut College's campus and other places around the globe where he had plucked up his ivy souvenirs. We were recipients of cuttings from *his* cuttings and to this day we have ivy plants that are thriving after all these years. These are descendants of slips which José brought back from his travels wrapped in damp Kleenex and stuffed in his pockets.

On one spring evening when we stopped at the farm we enjoyed the usual welcome: hospitality and great food and stimulating conversation. After copious wine, talk and hilarity, we went out to our car to drive home at a very early hour in the morning. As we pulled out on to the main road we were aware of an overpowering scent of lilacs. We soon discovered that the smell was coming from the back seat. José had crept out to our car sometime during the evening and had placed a huge bouquet of his lilacs there, along with a beautiful red serape acquired in Quito that my husband had admired.

These manifestations of his generosity joined the many others gifts that he and Pauline bestowed upon us over the years. One is my

José Limón, left, sitting on stone wall in front of his house at "the farm" in Stockton, New Jersey. Behind his right shoulder is the patio in which he grew ivies collected from his travels on tour. The Dance Collection, New York Public Library.

treasured silver bracelet which I have probably donned at least once a week for over forty years. Another is a day-glow magenta reboso which the Limóns gave me when we sailed to Europe in 1954. Friends who had come to wish us bon voyage and had remained on dock to watch the ocean liner move out into the river on its way toward Europe said that they could see me waving this vivid banner of color a long way down the Hudson River, long after people were no longer visible.

When Pauline was very sick but still able to get out to the country, José called us one early summer afternoon and asked if he could come to our house to see us. He had something which he wanted to give to us and would just drop it off before returning to care for Pauline. No, he could not stay for supper. An hour or so later I happened to look out from an upstairs window and saw José placing something on the stone terrace before coming around to knock on the door. The previous winter he taken down a large oak tree on the farm and, after letting it dry for eight months, was chopping up the wood. He came across a large wedge that had been the first cut into the tree and it reminded him of the shape of a thick slice of watermelon. Inspired, he took the wedge into one of the outbuildings on his property and started to paint it into the watermelon of his imagination. Vivid red-pink with a deep green rind and black seeds, it looked like a three-dimensional version of a Rufino Tamayo painting and a true evocation of Mexico. He was so excited with his handiwork, and knew that we would be too, so he brought it to us before the paint was even dry.

The last time I saw José was at Juilliard where he was rehearsing *Carlota* in one of the spacious new studios at Lincoln Center. Though seriously ill, he was still working to complete what he must have known was to be his last dance. Pauline had already made her final exit a year earlier and he did not have many more weeks to live. During a break in the rehearsal we spoke. He was still his gracious self and focused more on me than on himself. I had brought him a present of a rooted cutting from one of his gifts of ivy from Florence. I wanted him to know that the manifestations and remnants of friendship endure in living things. The delight in plants and gardens was something we all shared and I wanted to give back to him a plant that was a descendant from the original he had given to us so many years before. Not only do his ivies survive and flourish but his choreographic treasures continue to endure and move us. Fifty years after first encountering José, I know how much he influenced my life and how grateful I am that he did.

APPENDIX I
JOSÉ LIMÓN CHRONOLOGY

Compiled by Norton Owen

1908   José Arcadio Limón is born on January 12, in Culiacán, Mexico.

1915   Limón family moves to Tucson, Arizona, then later to Los Angeles.

1926   Graduates from Lincoln High School and enters UCLA as an art major.

1928   Moves to New York City to study at the New York School of Design.

1929   Sees dance performance by Harald Kreutzberg and Yvonne Georgi and decides to become a dancer, enrolling in the Humphrey-Weidman school.

1930   Appears in *Lysistrata* on Broadway in production choreographed by Doris Humphrey and Charles Weidman. Creates his first dance, *Etude in D Minor*, a duet with Letitia Ide.

1931   Forms The Little Group with Letitia Ide, Eleanor King and Ernestine Stodelle.

1932   Appears in the musical revue *Americana* on Broadway, featuring dances from Humphrey-Weidman repertoire.

1933   Appears in Irving Berlin's *As Thousands Cheer* on Broadway, choreographed by Charles Weidman. Choreographs Jerome Kern's *Roberta* (featuring Bob Hope) at Broadway's New Amsterdam Theatre.

1935   Appears in Humphrey's *New Dance* at Bennington School of the Dance.

1936   Appears in Humphrey's *Theatre Piece* and *With My Red Fires*, and Weidman's *Quest*.

1937   Selected as one of the first three Bennington Fellows.

1938   Appears in Humphrey's *Passacaglia and Fugue in C Minor*.

1939   Creates first major choreographic work, *Danzas Mexicanas*, at Mills College (Bennington Festival).

1940   Appears as featured dancer in Broadway's *Keep Off the Grass*, choreographed by George Balanchine. After breaking ties with Charles Weidman, leaves Humphrey-Weidman Company to work with May O'Donnell, with whom he creates *War Lyrics*.

1941   Co-Choreographs *Curtain Raiser, This Story is Legend* and *Three Inventories on Casey Jones* with May O'Donnell. Marries Pauline Lawrence on October 3.

1942   Dissolves partnership with May O'Donnell. Creates *Chaconne* for all-Bach program at Humphrey-Weidman Studio Theatre. Final appearance in a Broadway show, partnering Mary Ellen Moylan in Balanchine's *Rosalinda*.

1943   Appears in Humphrey/Limón dances on American and folk themes at Studio Theatre. Drafted into Army in April.

1944   Choreographs several works for U.S. Army Special Services, collaborating with composers Frank Loesser and Alex North.

1945   Debut of Trio with Beatrice Seckler and Dorothy Bird, directed by Humphrey. Choreographs *Concerto Grosso*. Discharged from Army in December.

1946   Attains American citizenship. Formal debut of José Limón Dance Company at Bennington College. Creates roles in Humphrey's *Lament for Ignacio Sanchez Mejias* and *The Story of Mankind*.

1947   Limón Company makes its New York debut at the Belasco Theatre on January 5. Creates lead role in Humphrey's *Day on Earth*.

1948   Limón Company appears at the first Connecticut College American Dance Festival, where it remains in residence each summer until 1973.

1949   Choreographs *The Moor's Pavane* and *La Malinche*.

1950   Appears in Paris with Ruth Page in the spring, becoming the first American modern dance company to appear in Europe. First tour to Mexico in the fall. Choreographs *The Exiles*. Receives Dance Magazine Award for *The Moor's Pavane* as the year's most outstanding choreography.

1951   Joins faculty of The Juilliard School's new dance division. Accepts invitation to Mexico City's Instituto Nacional de Bellas Artes, where he creates six works including *Tonantzintla, Dialogues* and *Los Cuatros Soles*.

1953   Creates roles in Humphrey's *Ruins and Visions* and *Ritmo Jondo*. Choreographs *The Visitation*.

1954   Choreographs *The Traitor*. Inaugurates U.S. State Department's International Exchange Program with Company tour to South America.

1955   Choreographs *Scherzo* and *Symphony for Strings*.

1956   Choreographs *There is a Time*, with Pulitzer Prize-winning score by Norman Dello Joio, and *The Emperor Jones*, with a commissioned score by Heitor Villa-Lobos.

1957   Embarks on a five-month Company tour of Europe and the Near East. Receives second Dance Magazine Award.

1958   Assumes the role of Artistic Director of the Limón Company upon the death of Doris Humphrey. Choreographs *Missa Brevis* and *Mazurkas*.

1960   Choreographs *Barren Sceptre* with Pauline Koner, based on the story of Macbeth. Leads the Company on a twelve-week State Department tour to South and Central America. Receives honorary doctorate from Wesleyan University.

1962   Limón Company opens the first dance performance at the New York Shakespeare Festival's Delacorte Theater in Central Park.

1963   Tours the Far East for twelve weeks with the Company under the sponsorship of the U.S. State Department. Creates *The Demon* to a score by Paul Hindemith, with the composer conducting the premiere.

1964   Creates *A Choreographic Offering* in tribute to Doris Humphrey. Receives the Capezio Award. Appointed as Artistic Director of the American Dance Theatre at Lincoln Center.

1965   Appears in nationally-telecast NET special, *The Dance Theater of José Limón*.

1966   Creates *The Winged*. Performs with the Company at the Washington Cathedral. Receives his first government funding, a $23,000 grant from the National Endowment for the Arts.

1967   Choreographs *Psalm*. Performs *The Moor's Pavane* (with the original cast) at the White House for President Johnson and King Hassan II of Morocco. Receives honorary doctorate from Colby College. Undergoes first of several operations for prostate cancer.

1968   Establishes the José Limón Dance Foundation as a not-for-profit corporation. Receives honorary doctorate from University of North Carolina.

1969   Appears for the last time onstage as a dancer, performing The Leader in *The Traitor* and The Moor in *The Moor's Pavane* at Brooklyn Academy of Music.

1970   *The Unsung* is premiered as a work in progress.

1971   Creates *Dances for Isadora*. Receives honorary doctorate from Oberlin College. Pauline Lawrence Limón dies.

1972   Choreographs *Orfeo* and *Carlota*. Films a solo dance interpretation of Martin Luther for CBS television. José Limón dies of cancer on December 2, at the age of 64.

1973   Limón Company tours to Soviet Union, becoming the first American modern dance company to survive its founder. The José Limón Collection is given to the New York Public Library Dance Collection by Charles Tomlinson.

1984   Daniel Lewis's *The Illustrated Dance Technique of José Limón* is published by Harper & Row.

1986   The José Limón Dance Foundation is authorized by Limón's heirs as the official legal entity to license José Limón's dances to other companies.

1989   Limón is named as a posthumous recipient of the Samuel H. Scripps/American Dance Festival Award, along with Doris Humphrey and Charles Weidman.

1993   Barbara Pollack's *Dance Is a Moment: A Portrait of José Limón in Words and Pictures* is published by Princeton Books. Larry Warren begins research for a biography of José Limón.

1994   The José Limón Dance Foundation publishes *A Catalogue of Dances* and the inaugural issues of *The Limón Journal*.

1995   Ann Vachon begins work on a José Limón documentary.

1996   A commemorative exhibition, *The Dance Heroes of José Limón*, is mounted at the New York Public Library for the Performing Arts.

96–97 The Limón Dance Company celebrates its 50th anniversary.

1997   José Limón is inducted into the National Museum of Dance Hall of Fame.

1998   *An Unfinished Memoir*, by José Limón is published by Wesleyan University Press. Video Artists International releases three classic Limón dances on home video with their original casts.

SOURCES FOR CHRONOLOGY

King, Eleanor. *Transformations*. Brooklyn, NY: Dance Horizons, 1978.

Kriegsman, Sali Ann. *Modern Dance in America: The Bennington Years*. Boston: G. K. Hall & Company, 1981.

Lewis, Daniel. *The Illustrated Dance Technique of José Limón*. New York: Harper & Row, 1984.

Pollack, Barbara and Charles Humphrey Woodford. *Dance is a Moment: A Portrait of José Limón in Words and Pictures*. Pennington, NJ: Princeton Book Company, 1993.

Siegel, Marcia B. *Days on Earth: The Dance of Doris Humphrey*. New Haven & London: Yale University Press, 1987.

APPENDIX II

CHRONOLOGICAL LIST OF WORKS CHOREOGRAPHED BY JOSÉ LIMÓN

Compiled by Lynn Garafola

This chronology is a shortened version of the list appearing in *José Limón: An Unfinished Memoir* edited by Lynn Garafola and published in 1998 by Wesleyan University Press in the series *Studies in Dance History*.

Since Limón's early works were first shown at studio performances or group concerts for which few programs survive, it is extremely difficult to establish accurate premiere dates. It is likely that several of the pre-1935 works listed below actually premiered before the dates given for them.

Etude in D-Flat Major
Music: Alexander Scriabin
Premiere: December 1930, Humphrey-Weidman Studio, New York

Bacchanale (with Eleanor King and Ernestine Henoch*)
Music: percussion accompaniment
Premiere: December 1930, Humphrey-Weidman Studio, New York
*Later known as Ernestine Stodelle.

Petite Suite (with Eleanor King and Ernestine Henoch)
Music: Claude Debussy
Premiere: spring 1931, Humphrey-Weidman Studio, New York

Tango (also called *Tango Rhythms*)
Music: percussion score by José Limón
Costumes: Charles Weidman
Premiere: spring 1931, Humphrey-Weidman Studio, New York

B Minor Suite (also called *Polonaise, Rondeau, Badinerie* and *Suite in B Minor*)
Music: Johann Sebastian Bach
Premiere: spring 1931, St. Bartholomew Community House, New York

Mazurka (with Eleanor King)
Music: Alexander Scriabin
Premiere: spring 1931, St. Bartholomew Community House, New York

Two Preludes (solo)
Music: Reginald de Koven
Company: Little Group
Premiere: 7 August 1931, Westport Barn Theatre, Westport, Conn.

Danza (solo)
Music: Sergei Prokofiev
Company: Little Group
Premiere: 18 October 1931, Sharon, Conn.

Roberta
Musical comedy in two acts.
Book and lyrics: Otto Harbach
Music: Jerome Kern
Producer: Max Gordon
Sets: Clark Robinson
Costumes: Kiviette
Premiere: 18 November 1933, New Amsterdam Theatre, New York
Note: Limón, who did not receive a general credit, choreographed *Blue Shadows*, a group number that came near the end of the first act.

Canción y Danza (also called *Dance*) (solo)
Music: Federico Mompou
Premiere: 30 April 1933, Studio 61, Carnegie Hall, New York

Pièces Froides (solo) (also called *Trois Pièces Froides*)
Music: Erik Satie
Premiere: 30 April 1933, Studio 61, Carnegie Hall, New York

1935 (dance-drama)
Premiere: summer 1935, Perry-Mansfield Camp, Steamboat Springs, Colorado

Three Studies (solo)
Music: Carl Engel
Company: Charles Weidman and Group
Premiere: 12 October 1935, Washington Irving High School, New York

Nostalgic Fragments
Music: Igor Stravinsky (*Suite pour petit orchestre*, no. 2)
Costumes: Charles Weidman
Premiere: 22 December 1935, Adelphi Theatre, New York

Prelude
Music: Francis Poulenc (from *Aubade*)
Costumes: Charles Weidman
Premiere: 22 December 1935, Adelphi Theatre, New York

Satiric Lament
Music: Francis Poulenc (from *Aubade*)
Premiere: 26 February 1936, New School for Social Research, New York

Hymn (solo)
Music: percussion
Costume: José Limón
Premiere: 15 March 1936, Majestic Theatre, New York

Danza de la Muerte (Dance of Death)
Music: Henry Clark (*Saraband for the Dead, Saraband for the Living*),
   Norman Lloyd (*Interlude*)
Scenery: Gerard Gentile
Costumes: Betty Joiner
Premiere: 12 August 1937, Vermont State Armory, Bennington, Vt.

Opus for Three and Props
Music: Dmitri Shostakovitch
Scenery: Gerard Gentile
Costumes: Betty Joiner
Premiere: 12 August 1937, Vermont State Armory, Bennington, Vt.

Danzas Mexicanas (also called *Suite of Dances About Mexico*)
Music: Lionel Nowak
Costumes: Pauline Lawrence
Premiere: 4 August 1939, Lisser Hall, Mills College, Oakland, Cal.

Three Preludes (solo)
Music: Frédéric Chopin
Premiere: 11 February 1940, Genevieve Jones Studio, Pittsburgh, Penn.

War Lyrics
Music: Esther Williamson
Text: William Archibald
Scenery: Gyorgy and Juliet Kepes
Costumes: José Limón
Company: José Limón and Group
Premiere: 27 July 1940, Lisser Hall, Mills College, Oakland, Cal.

Curtain Raiser (with May O'Donnell)
Music: Ray Green
Scenery: Claire Falkenstein
Premiere: 25 February 1941, Fresno State Auditorium, Fresno, Cal.

This Story is Legend (with May O'Donnell)
Music: Ray Green
Spoken text: William Carlos Williams (*In the American Grain*)
Scenery and costumes: Claire Falkenstein
Premiere: 25 February 1941, Fresno State College Auditorium, Fresno,
  Cal.

Praeludium: *Theme and Variations* (with May O'Donnell)
Music: Ray Green
Premiere: 25 February 1941, Fresno State College Auditorium, Fresno,
  Cal.

Three Inventories on Casey Jones (with May O'Donnell)
A Fantasy.
Music: Ray Green
Decor: Claire Falkenstein
Premiere: 25 February 1941, Fresno State College Auditorium, Fresno,
  Cal.

Alley Tune (with Helen Ellis)
Music: David Guion
Premiere: 30 July 1942, Gunter Hall, Colorado College, Colorado Springs,
  Colo.

Turkey in the Straw (solo)
Music: traditional (arranged by David Guion)
Premiere: 30 July 1942, Gunter Hall, Colorado College, Colorado Springs,
  Colo.

Mazurka
Music: Frédéric Chopin
Premiere: 30 July 1942, Gunter Hall, Colorado College, Colorado Springs,
  Colo.

Chaconne (also called *Chaconne in D Minor*) (solo)
Music: Johann Sebastian Bach (from *Sonata in D Minor for Unaccompanied
  Violin*)
Costume: Pauline Lawrence
Company: Doris Humphrey and the Hunphrey-Weidman Repertory
  Company
Premiere: 27 December 1942

Western Folk Suite
Music: Norman Cazden (*Reel*, after a song by Woody Guthrie), Charles
  Ives (*Ballad of Charlie Rutlage*), traditional (*Pop Goes the Weasel*, arranged
  by Esther Williamson)

Costumes: Pauline Lawrence
Company: José Limón and the Hunphrey-Weidman Repertory Company
Premiere: 11 March 1943, Humphrey-Weidman Studio Theatre, New
  York

Fun for the Birds
Lyrics: Brace Conning, John Shubert, William Galbraith
Music: Arthur Schwartz, Wadsworth Douglas
Stage director: Don Stevens
Premiere: 5 September 1943, Mosque Theatre, Richmond, Va.
Note: Limón shared dance direction credit for this U.S. Army show with
  Thomas Knox.

Spanish Dance
Music: Manuel de Falla
Costumes: Pauline Lawrence
Company: Camp Lee Concert Dance Group
Premiere: 13 February 1944, Mosque Theatre, Richmond, Va.

Interlude Dances
Music: Roy Harris (*Folk Symphony*)
Company: Camp Lee Concert Dance Group
Premiere: 13 February 1944, Mosque Theatre, Richmond, Va.

Rosenkavalier Waltz
Music: Richard Strauss
Costumes: Pauline Lawrence
Company: Camp Lee Concert Dance Group
Premiere: 13 February 1944, Mosque Theatre, Richmond, Va.

Mexilinda
Music: Sergei Rachmaninoff, Nikolai Rimsky-Korsakov, Norman Carden,
  Manuel Infante, Darius Milhaud, Manuel de Falla, Johannes Brahms,
  Johann Strauss
Costumes: Pauline Lawrence
Premiere: 20 February 1944, Service Club 1, Camp Lee, Va.

Deliver the Goods (A Quartermaster Corps Musical Revue)
Producer: Don Stevens
Book: Sidney Abel, John Thompson, Barry Farnol, Don Stevens
Music: Frank Hundertmark
Sets: Albert Rubens, Barry Farnol
Stage direction: Ray Hinkley, William Howell

Musical direction: Henry Aaron
Premiere: 27 April 1944, Camp Lee, Va.

Song of the Medics
Book, music, and lyrics: Philip Freedman, Charles Broffman
Sets: Perry Watkins
Stage direction: Walter Armitage
Musical direction: George Kleinsinger
Costumes: Rowena Fairchild
Premiere: 2 July 1944, Fort Dix, N.J.

Hi, Yank!
Music and lyrics: Frank Loesser, Alex North, Jack Hill, Jesse Berkman
Sets and costumes: Robert T. Stevenson, Al Hamilton
Premiere: [August?] 1944, Fort Dix, N.J.

Concerto (later called *Concerto Grosso*)
Music: Antonio Vivaldi (sometimes "Vivaldi-Bach")
Costumes: Pauline Lawrence
Premiere: 11 April 1945, Clifford Scott High School, East Orange, N.J.
Note: This performance marked the debut of the group that was the
    immediate forerunner of the José Limón Dance Company.

Eden Tree
Music: Carl Engel, José Limón
Costumes: Pauline Lawrence
Premiere: 11 April 1945, Clifford Scott High School, East Orange, N.J.

Three Ballads
Music: traditional (Kentucky mountain ballad), Charles Ives (*Ballad of
    Charlie Rutlage*), traditional (arranged by Elie Siegmeister)
Costumes: Pauline Lawrence
Premiere: 19 May 1945, Studio Theatre, New York

Danza (solo)
Music: J. Arcadio
Costume: Pauline Lawrence
Premiere: 6 September 1946, Jacob's Pillow, Beckett, Mass.
Note: J. Arcadio was probably a pseudonym for Limón, whose middle
    name was Arcadio.

Masquerade (solo)
Music: Sergei Prokofiev (Sonata no. 5 in C Major, op. 38)
Costume: Pauline Lawrence
Premiere: 29 November 1946, Howard Hall, St. Louis, Mo.

The Song of Songs
Music: Lukas Foss
Costumes: Pauline Lawrence
Premiere: 19 August 1947, Hatch Memorial Shell, Charles River
 Esplanade, Boston, Mass.

Sonata Opus 4
Music: Johann Sebastian Bach
Premiere: 19 August 1947, Hatch Memorial Shell, Charles River
 Esplanade, Boston, Mass.

La Malinche
Music: Norman Lloyd
Costumes: Pauline Lawrence
Company: José Limón and Company
Premiere: 24 March 1949, Jordan Hall, Boston, Mass.

The Moor's Pavane
Variations on the Theme of Othello.
Music: Henry Purcell, arranged by Simon Sadoff
Costumes: Pauline Lawrence
Company: José Limón and Company
Premiere: 17 August 1949, Palmer Auditorium, Connecticut College,
 New London, Conn.

The Exiles
Music: Arnold Schoenberg (Chamber Symphony no. 2, op. 38)
Scenery: Anita Weschler
Costumes: Pauline Lawrence
Company: José Limón and Company
Premiere: 11 August 1950, Palmer Auditorium, Connecticut College,
 New London, Conn.

Concert
Music: Johann Sebastian Bach (preludes and fugues, arranged by Simon
 Sadoff)
Costumes: Pauline Lawrence
Company: José Limón and Company
Premiere: 19 August 1950, Palmer Auditorium, Connecticut College,
 New London, Conn.

Los cuatro soles (The Four Suns)
Music: Carlos Chávez
Libretto: Carlos Chávez, Miguel Covarrubias

Sets and costumes: Miguel Covarrubias
Company: Academia de la Danza Mexicana (augmented by members of
   the Ballet Nacional
Premiere: 31 March 1951, Palacio de Bellas Artes, Mexico City

Tonantzintla
Music: Antonio Soler (orchestrated by Rodolfo Halffter)
Scenery and costumes: Miguel Covarrubias
Company: Academia de la Danza Mexicana
Premiere: 31 March 1951, Palacio de Bellas Artes, Mexico City

Diálogos (also called *Dialogues*)
Music: Norman Lloyd
Scenery and costumes: Julio Prieto
Premiere: April 1951, Palacio de Bellas Artes, Mexico City

Antígona (Antigone)
Music: Carlos Chávez
Sets and costumes: Miguel Covarrubias
Prologue: Salvador Novo
Company: Academia de la Danza Mexicana
Premiere: 24 November 1951, Palacio de Bellas Artes, Mexico City

Redes (Nets)
Music: Silvestre Revueltas (from the film *The Wave*)
Libretto: José Revueltas
Sets and costumes: Department of Theatrical Production, Academia de la
   Danza, Mexico City
Company: Academia de la Danza Mexicana
Premiere: 8 December 1951, Palacio de Bellas Artes, Mexico City
Note: *El Grito* (1952) was a revised version of this work.

The Queen's Epicedium
Music: Henry Purcell (*Elegy on the Death of Queen Mary*)
Costumes: Pauline Lawrence
Company: José Limón and Dance Company
Premiere: 21 August 1952, Palmer Auditorium, Connecticut College,
   New London, Conn.

The Visitation
Music: Arnold Schoenberg (Piano Pieces, op. 11)
Costumes: Pauline Lawrence
Company: José Limón and Dance Company

Premiere: 23 August 1952, Palmer Auditorium, Connecticut College, New London, Conn.

El Grito (The Shout)
Music: Silvestre Revueltas (from the film *The Wave*)
Libretto: José Revueltas
Costumes: Consuelo Gana
Company: José Limón and Dance Company
Premiere: 5 December 1952, Juilliard Concert Hall, New York
Note: The Limón company was augmented by dancers from other companies and students from Limón's classes at the Dance Players Studio.

Don Juan Fantasia
Music: Franz Liszt
Costumes: Pauline Lawrence
Company: José Limón and Dance Company
Premiere: 22 August 1953, Palmer Auditorium, Connecticut College, New London, Conn.

Ode to the Dance
Music: Samuel Barber (*Capricorn Concerto*, op. 21)
Scenery: Paul Trautvetter
Costumes: Pauline Lawrence
Company: José Limón and Dance Company
Premiere: 29 January 1954, Juilliard Concert Hall, New York

The Traitor
Music: Gunther Schuller (*Symphony for Brasses*)
Scenery: Paul Trautvetter
Costumes: Pauline Lawrence
Company: José Limón and Dance Company
Premiere: 19 August 1954, Palmer Auditorium, Connecticut College, New London, Conn.

Scherzo
Music: John Barracuda, Stoddard Lincoln, Lucy Venable (percussion improvisation)
Company: students from The Juilliard School Dance Division
Premiere: 11 May 1955, Juilliard School of Music, New York
Note: This was a study of a work presented in the summer at the American Dance Festival.

Scherzo
Music: Hazel Johnson (percussion score)
Costumes: Pauline Lawrence
Company: José Limón and Dance Company

Premiere: 19 August 1955, Palmer Auditorium, Connecticut College, New London, Conn.

Symphony for Strings
Music: William Schuman
Costumes: Pauline Lawrence
Company: José Limón and Dance Company
Premiere: 19 August 1955, Palmer Auditorium, Connecticut College, New London, Conn.

Variations on a Theme (later called *There is a Time*)
Music: Norman Dello Joio (*Meditations on Ecclesiastes*)
Costumes: Pauline Lawrence
Company: José Limón Dance Company
Premiere: 20 April 1956, Juilliard Concert Hall, New York

King's Heart
Music: Stanley Wolfe
Scenery: Durevol Quitzow
Costumes: Pauline Lawrence
Company: Juilliard Dance Theater
Premiere: 27 April 1956, Juilliard Concert Hall, New York

The Emperor Jones
Dance-drama after the play of Eugene O'Neill.
Music: Heitor Villa-Lobos
Scenery: Kim Edgar Swados
Costumes: Pauline Lawrence
Company: José Limón and Company
Premiere: 12 July 1956, Empire State Music Festival, Ellenville, N.Y.

Rhythmic Study
Music: self-accompanied
Company: members of the José Limón Company
Premiere: 12 December 1956, Juilliard School of Music, New York

Blue Roses
A choreographic fantasy based on *The Glass Menagerie*, by Tennessee Williams.
Music: William Lorin (based on themes of Paul Bowles)
Costumes: Pauline Lawrence
Company: José Limón and Dance Company
Premiere: 16 August 1957, Palmer Auditorium, Connecticut College, New London, Conn.

Missa Brevis
Music: Zoltán Kodály (*Missa Brevis in Tempore Belli*)
Projection and costumes: Ming Cho Lee
Company: Juilliard Dance Theater (with members of the José Limón Company)
Premiere: 11 April 1958, Juilliard Concert Hall, New York

Seranata
Music: Paul Bowles
Scenery: Thomas Watson
Costumes: Pauline Lawrence
Company: José Limón and Dance Company
Premiere: 14 August 1958, Palmer Auditorium. Connecticut College, New London, Conn.

Dances (in honor of Poznan, Wroclaw, Katowice, and Warszawa)
Music: Frédéric Chopin
Costumes: Lavina Nielsen
Company: José Limón and Dance Company
Premiere: 15 August 1958, Palmer Auditorium, Connecticut College, New London, Conn.
Note: Limón later presented a shortened version of this work under the title *Mazurkas*.

Tenebrae, 1914
Episodes in the life of Edith Cavell.
Music: John Wilson
Scenery: Ming Cho Lee
Costumes: Pauline Lawrence
Company: José Limón and Dance Company
Premiere: 13 August 1959, Palmer Auditorium, Connecticut College, New London, Conn.

The Apostate
Music: Ernst Krenek (*Elegy for Strings*)
Scenery: Ming Cho Lee
Costumes: Pauline Lawrence
Company: José Limón and Dance Company
Premiere: 15 August 1959, Palmer Auditorium, Connecticut College, New London, Conn.

Barren Sceptre (with Pauline Koner)
Music: Gunther Schuller
Costumes: Pauline Lawrence

Company: José Limón and Dance Company
Premiere: 8 April 1960, Juilliard Concert Hall, New York

Performance (Over the Footlights and Back)
Variations on a Theme of William Schuman.
Music: Hugh Aitken, William Bergsma, Jacob Druckman, Vittorio Giannini, Norman Lloyd, Vincent Persichetti, Robert Starer, and Hugo Weisgall
Company: Juilliard Dance Ensemble
Premiere: 14 April 1961, Juilliard Concert Hall, New York

The Moirai (The Fates)
Music: Hugh Aitken
Costumes: Pauline Lawrence
Company: José Limón and Dance Company
Premiere: 18 August 1961, Palmer Auditorium, Connecticut College, New London, Conn.

I, Odysseus
Music: Hugh Aitken
Costumes: Nellie Hatfield, Elizabeth Parsons
Company: José Limón and Dance Company
Properties: Thomas Watson, William McIver
Premiere: 18 August 1962, Palmer Auditorium, Connecticut College, New London, Conn.

Sonata for Two Cellos (solo)
Music: Meyer Kupferman
Costumes: Pauline Lawrence
Premiere: 19 August 1961, Palmer Auditorium, Connecticut College, New London, Conn.

The Demon
Music: Paul Hindemith
Scenery and costumes: Malcolm McCormick
Company: José Limón Company
Premiere: 13 March 1963, Juilliard Concert Hall, New York

Concerto in D Minor After Vivaldi
Music: Johann Sebastian Bach
Costumes: Pauline Lawrence
Company: Juilliard Dance Ensemble
Premiere: 10 May 1963, Juilliard Concert Hall, New York

Two Essays for Large Ensemble
Music: Johann Sebastian Bach (excerpts from *A Musical Offering*)

Company: Juilliard Dance Ensemble
Premiere: 17 April 1964, Juilliard Concert Hall, New York

A Choreographic Offering
Music: Johann Sebastian Bach (*A Musical Offering*)
Costumes: Pauline Lawrence
Company: José Limón and Dance Company (augmented by American
  Dance Festival students)
Premiere: 15 August 1964, Palmer Auditorium, Connecticut College,
  New London, Conn.

Variations on a Theme of Paganini
Music: Johannes Brahms (excerpts from *Variations on a Theme of Paganini*,
  op. 35)
Costumes: Charles D. Tomlinson
Company: Juilliard Dance Ensemble
Premiere: 12 February 1965, Juilliard Concert Hall, New York

Dance Suite
Music: Sergei Prokofiev
Costumes: Linda Zaslow
Company: Brooklyn College Modern Dance Club
Premiere: 7 May 1965, George Gershwin Theatre, Brooklyn College,
  New York

My Son, My Enemy
Music: Vivian Fine
Costumes: Pauline Lawrence, Charles D. Tomlinson
Company: José Limón and Company
Premiere: 14 August 1965, Palmer Auditorium, Connecticut College,
  New London, Conn.

The Winged
Music: Hank Johnson (incidental music)
Costumes: Pauline Lawrence
Company: José Limón and Company
Premiere: 20 August 1966, Palmer Auditorium, Connecticut College,
  New London, Conn.

MacAber's Dance
Music: Jacob Druckman (*Animus I for Trombone and Electronic Tape*)
Company: Juilliard Dance Ensemble
Premiere: 20 April 1967, Juilliard Concert Hall, New York

Psalm
Music: Eugene Lester
Costumes: Pauline Lawrence
Company: José Limón and Company
Premiere: 19 August 1967, Palmer Auditorium, Connecticut College, New London, Conn.

Comedy
Music: Josef Wittman
Company: José Limón and Company
Premiere: 10 August 1968, Palmer Auditorium, Connecticut College, New London, Conn.

Legend
Music: music for tape selected by Simon Sadoff
Company: José Limón and Company
Premiere: 17 August 1968, Palmer Auditorium, Connecticut College, New London, Conn.

La Piñata
Music: Burrill Phillips
Scenery: Douglas Schmidt
Costumes: Pauline Lawrence, Betty Williams
Company: Juilliard Dance Ensemble
Premiere: 20 March 1969, Juilliard Concert Hall, New York

The Unsung (Work in Progress)
"Pantheon: Metacomet, Pontiac, Tecumseh, Red Eagle, Black Hawk, Osceola, Sitting Bull, Geronimo."
Music: danced in silence
Costumes: Charles D. Tomlinson
Company: Juilliard School Dance Division
Premiere: 26 May 1970, Juilliard Theater, New York
Note: The finished work premiered the following year.

And David Wept
Music: Joe Darion, Ezra Laderman
Scenery: Neil DeLuca
Producer: Pamela Ilott
Director: Jerry Schnur
Musical director: Alfredo Antonini
Premiere: WCBS-TV News Special, 11 April 1971

Revel
Music: Elizabeth Sawyer (Woodwind Quintet)

Costumes: Charles D. Tomlinson
Company: Juilliard Dance Ensemble
Premiere: 5 May 1971, Juilliard Theater, New York

Yerma
An Opera in Three Acts.
Music: Heitor Villa-Lobos
Libretto: Federico García Lorca
Stage direction: Basil Langton
Scenery and costumes: Allen Charles Klein
Original paintings: Giorgio de Chirico
Conductor: Christopher Keene
Company: Santa Fe Opera
Premiere: 12 August 1971, Santa Fe, New Mexico

The Unsung
"Pantheon: Metacomet, Pontiac, Tecumseh, Red Eagle, Black Hawk, Osceola, Sitting Bull, Geronimo."
Music: danced in silence
Costumes: Charles D. Tomlinson
Company: Juilliard Dance Ensemble
Premiere: 5 November 1971, Walnut Street Theatre, Philadelphia, Penn.

Isadora (Five Visions of Isadora Duncan) (also called *Dance for Isadora* [Five Evocations – in Homage] or *Dances for Isadora* [Five Evocations of Isadora Duncan])
Music: Frédéric Chopin
Costumes: Charles D. Tomlinson
Company: José Limón Dance Company
Premiere: 10 December 1971, Cleveland Museum of Art, Cleveland, Ohio

The Wind (new work in progress)
Music: Joseph Castaldo (*Kaleidoscope*)
Company: Philadelphia Dance Theatre
Premiere: 17 December 1971, Philadelphia Musical Academy, Penn.

Orfeo
Music: Ludwig van Beethoven (op. 95, no. 11 in F Minor)
Costumes: Charles D. Tomlinson
Company: José Limón Dance Company
Premiere: 2 October 1972, ANTA Theater, New York

Carlota
Music: danced in silence
Costumes: Charles D. Tomlinson

Company: José Limón Dance Company
Premiere: 5 October 1972, ANTA Theater, New York

Waldstein Sonata (with Daniel Lewis)
Music: Ludwig van Beethoven (Piano Sonata no. 21)
Costumes: Robert Yodice
Company: Juilliard Dance Ensemble
Premiere: 26 April 1975, Juilliard Theater, New York
Program note: "José Limón worked with his company on 'The Waldstein
  Sonata' in the winter of 1971. The work has been reconstructed and
  completed by Daniel Lewis."

Luther
Music: Ezra Laderman
Scenery: Tom John
Costumes: Charles D. Tomlinson
Producer: Pamela Ilott
Director: Jerome Schnur
Premiere: 26 October 1986, WCBS-TV, *For Our Times* series,
Note: Recorded in 1972, the film was set aside after Limóns death later
  that year and lost for more than a decade. In 1986 the footage was
  edited for broadcast.

General Note: During Limón's career, various names were used for his
companies.

APPENDIX III
ALPHABETICAL LIST OF WORKS CHOREOGRAPHED BY JOSÉ LIMÓN

A Choreographic Offering	1964
And David Wept	1971
Alley Tune	1942
Antigona	1951
Bacchanale	1930
Barren Sceptre	1960
B Minor Suite	1931
Blue Roses	1957
Cancíon y Danza	1933
Carlota	1972
Chaconne	1942
Comedy	1968
Concert	1950
Concerto (later called *Concerto Grosso*)	1945
Concerto in D Minor After Vivaldi	1963
Curtain Raiser	1941
Dances (later called *Mazurkas*)	1958
Dance Suite	1965
Danza	1931
Danza	1946
Danza de la Muerte	1937
Danzas Mexicanas	1939
Deliver the Goods	1944
Diálogos	1951
Don Juan Fantasia	1953
Eden Tree	1945
El Grito (Revised version of *Redes*)	1952
Etude in D-flat Major	1930
Fun for the Birds	1943
Hi, Yank	1944
Hymn	1936
Interlude Dances	1944
I, Odysseus	1962
Isadora (also called *Dances for Isadora*)	1971

King's Heart	1956
La Malinche	1949
La Piñata	1969
Legend	1968
Los Cuatros Soles	1951
Luther	1986
MacAber's Dance	1967
Masquerade	1946
Mazurka	1931
Mazurka	1942
Mazurkas	1958
Mexilinda	1944
Missa Brevis	1958
My Son, My Enemy	1965
1935	1935
Nostalgic Fragments	1935
Ode to the Dance	1954
Opus for Three and Props	1937
Orfeo	1972
Performance	1961
Petite Suite	1931
Pièces Froides	1933
Praeludium: Theme and Variations	1941
Prelude	1935
Psalm	1967
Redes	1951
Revel	1971
Rhythmic Study	1956
Roberta	1933
Rosenkavalier Waltz	1944
Satiric Lament	1936
Scherzo	1955
Scherzo (revised version)	1955
Serenata	1958
Sonata for Two Cellos	1961
Sonata Opus 4	1947
Song of Songs	1947
Song of the Medics	1944
Spanish Dance	1944
Symphony for Strings	1955
Tango	1931
Tenebrae, 1914	1959
The Apostate	1959

The Demon	1963
The Emperor Jones	1956
The Exiles	1950
The Moirai	1961
The Moor's Pavane	1949
The Queen's Epicedium	1952
The Traitor	1954
The Unsung (Work in Progress)	1970
The Unsung	1971
The Visitation	1952
The Wind (Work in Progress)	1971
The Winged	1966
This Story is Legend	1941
Three Ballads	1945
Three Studies	1935
Three Inventories on Casey Jones	1941
Three Preludes	1940
Tonantzintla	1951
Turkey in the Straw	1942
Two Essays for Large Ensemble	1964
Two Preludes	1931
Variations on a Theme (later called	1956
There is a Time)	
Variations on a Theme of Paganini	1965
Waldstein Sonata	1975
War Lyrics	1940
Western Folk Suite	1943
Yerma	1971

NOTES ON CONTRIBUTORS

Melinda Copel is completing her doctorate at Temple University in Philadelphia. Her current research explores the State Department sponsored tours of José Limón and his modern dance company, and the historical origins of Morris dance. She is assisting Ann Vachon, director of Dance Conduit, with research and grant writing to facilitate the production of a forthcoming video documentary on the life and work of José Limón. She studied at the Martha Graham School and performed for many years as part of the southern Vermont dance community.

June Dunbar began studying with José Limón in 1949 after receiving her BA from Vassar as a theater major. She studied choreography with Doris Humphrey and Louis Horst and performed in Humphrey's workshop performances in New York and, on occasions, with Limón when he worked with an expanded company. In 1953 she started to teach technique at Limón's studio. In the same year she joined the faculty at The Juilliard School where she remained until 1967. Teaching assignments took her to Amsterdam and Rotterdam and for several months she taught Limón technique in London as well as at colleges throughout the US. For the last ten years of her association with the Juilliard Dance Division, she also served as its Associate Director. From 1967 to 1972 she directed the Lincoln Center Student Program at Juilliard and in 1972 became Associate Director, then Artistic Director of the Lincoln Center Institute, the educational arm of Lincoln Center, where she remained until 1992. In addition to co-producing a documentary film about Bessie Schonberg, she has served as a consultant on projects related to the performing arts and education since 1992.

Lynn Garafola is the author of *Diaghilev's Ballets Russes*, translator of Marius Petipa's diaries, curator of the exhibition *Dance for a City: Fifty Years of New York City Ballet*, and editor, most recently, of *Rethinking the Sylph: New Perspectives on the Romantic Ballet* and *José Limón: An Unfinished Memoir*. A former Getty scholar and editor of the book series Studies in Dance History, she writes regularly for *Dance Magazine* and other publications. She holds a Ph.D. in Comparative Literature from the City University of New York.

Michael Hollander performed with the Limón Company from 1952 to 1958 in a number of dances including *Ode to the Dance, The Traitor, Ritmo Jondo, Ruins and Visions, Scherzo, There is a Time, The Emperor Jones, Dance Overture, Missa Brevis* and *Dances (Mazurkas)*. He was understudy for José's role in *The Moor's Pavane* and learned his solos in *The Lament for Ignacio Sanchez Mejias*. He also appeared, independently, in a duet with Miriam Pandor, choreographed by her, and a duet with Pearl Lang, choreographed by Sophie Maslow. He performed several of his own works including *Inventions*, which is based on "isolations" in Limón technique, and *Icarus*, in the Little Concert Series at Connecticut College in 1957. Michael (Mike) taught Limón technique at the Limón studio and at the Dance Department of the Juilliard School of Music. He was also instructor for José's class for men at Connecticut College. In addition, he taught at the Dance Circle in Boston and gave master classes at Smith, Wellesley, Barnard and other colleges. Michael was critic for *The New London Day* during the summer from 1955 through 1958 and an Associate Editor of *Dance Observer* in 1955 and 1956. He stopped dancing in 1958 and later became an architect. He has been teaching architectural history and theory at Pratt Institute in New York City since 1973.

Betty Jones is an internationally known authority on the Humphrey-Limón heritage. Her experience is a result of a distinguished association with her mentors José Limón and Doris Humphrey. In 1947 she became a founding member and principal dancer with the José Limón Dance Company, and during a period of over twenty years created a legacy of roles including Desdemona opposite Limón's Moor in his classic work *The Moor's Pavane*. With the company Ms. Jones danced at the White House, has appeared in television productions as well as performing worldwide. She served for two decades as a faculty member of The Juilliard School and the American Dance Festival. She is Co-Artistic Director of her own Dances We Dance Company and has taught throughout Europe, Russia, America and the Far East. She has re-staged Limón repertory for the Maly Opera Ballet in St. Petersburg. In 1993 she was recipient of the Balasaraswati/Joy Dewey Beineke Endowed Chair for Distinguished Teaching at the American Dance Festival.

Carla Maxwell joined the José Limón Dance Company in 1965. She soon became a principal dancer under Limón's direction and, in 1975, Assistant Artistic Director under Ruth Currier. In 1978, Ms. Maxwell was appointed Artistic Director of the José Limón Dance Company. Ms. Maxwell has staged Limón's work for many major companies and is also responsible for many of the Company's reconstructions. She received the 1995 *Dance Magazine* Award for her work with the Company as director, performer and master teacher of the Limón heritage. Ms. Maxwell dances many of the major roles with the Company, including the role of *Carlota*, Mr. Limón's final ballet, which he choreographed for her.

As choreographer, Ms. Maxwell has created works for regional companies throughout the US. She created *Sonata* for the Limón Company in October, 1980 and *Keeping Still, Mountain* in 1988 to Meredith Monk's *Dolmen Music*. Ms. Maxwell has taught nationally as a master teacher, and internationally as both a representative of the Limón Company and as a guest artist-in-residence.

Ann Murphy is a dance critic in the San Francisco Bay area who writes for the *East Bay Express*, the Alameda Newspaper Group, and is a regular contributor to *Dance Magazine*. She studied ballet at Margaret Craske's Manhattan School of Dance and in San Francisco with former Merce Cunningham dancer Brynar Mehl and performed in the Brynar Mehl Dance Company. She studied modern dance with Helen Priest Rogers, Andy Peck, Roberta Garrison, Marni and David Wood, Ellen Bromberg and Lucas Hoving. She was Hoving's manager from 1986 to 1990, has been editor for political as well as dance publications, a publicist and a fund-raiser. She is the mother of two young boys and lives in Berkeley, California.

Norton Owen is the Institute Director of the José Limón Dance Foundation, and Director of Preservation for Jacob's Pillow Dance Festival. At Limón he is responsible for licensing the works of José Limón to companies world-wide, maintaining the Institute's extensive archives and supervising all educational activities. At Jacob's Pillow, he initiates and conducts programs concerning dance documentation, exhibitions and archival resources. His book on the history of Jacob's Pillow, *A Certain Place*, was published in 1997. He served as curator of *The Dance Heroes of José Limón*, a major exhibition mounted by the New York Public Library for the Performing Arts which subsequently traveled to the National Museum of Dance in Saratoga Springs, New York. He has also organized major exhibitions about Paul Taylor, Merce Cunningham, Ted Shawn and Bronislava Nijinska. He has written articles for *Dance Magazine* and *Performing Arts Resources*, edited three issues of the *Limón Journal* and contributed an Afterword to the new publication of Limón's unfinished autobiography.

Sarah Stackhouse danced with the José Limón Company from 1958 to 1969 as a principal dancer and partner to Mr. Limón. She was featured in female roles of Limón's masterworks of that period. As well, she danced with American Repertory Theatre at Lincoln Center directed by Limón, The Alvin Ailey Dance Theater, Louis Falco and Featured Dancers, the Workgroup directed by Daniel Nagrin and Annabelle Gamson, Dance Solos, Inc. In addition to performing, she assisted Limón for many years in his classes and rehearsals at The Juilliard School and American Dance Festival. Returning to the Limón Company after twenty years, she now stages, coaches and directs many of the works in the repertory. She has staged and directed Limón's works on many numerous companies including the Paris Opera Ballet, Nureyev and Friends, national ballet companies in Prague, Mexico City, Mulhouse, France; in the US for Ohio Ballet, Cleveland Ballet, Dance Theatre of Harlem and for Mikail Baryshnikov. Ms. Stackhouse has taught at The Juilliard School, American Dance Festival and Purchase College Conservatory. As master teacher she has conducted residencies in the US, Europe and the Far East.

Jennifer Tipton is well known for her work in theater, dance and opera. Most recently she has lit *Beatrice and Benedict* for the Santa Fe Opera and *The Rake's Progress* at the Metropolitan Opera. Her recent work in dance includes Twyla Tharp's *Roy's Joys* and *The Storyteller* for the Australian Ballet and Trisha Brown's *Canto Pianto*. In theater: Euripides, *The Iphigenia Cycle* at the Court Theater in Chicago and the Wooster Group's production of *Houselights*. Future productions include designing the light for Sam Shepard's *Eyes for Consuela* at the Manhattan Theater Club and Brecht's *Galileo* at the Yale Repertory Theater. Ms. Tipton also teaches lighting at the Yale School of Drama.

Charles D. Tomlinson grew up in Winston Salem, North Carolina and received his BA in Theater Arts at the University of Miami in scenic and costume design. Graduate study took him to London where he spent two years at the Slade School. He appeared as a performer in both dance and theater in London and New York. His many scenic and costume design credits include work for both ballet and modern dance companies, including the Limón Company, the Louisville Ballet, the Pennsylvania Ballet, Valerie Bettis Company, the London Festival Ballet, Norman Walker's company, The Juilliard School and the Boston Ballet. He has also worked with choreographers as diverse as Antony Tudor, Anna Sokolow, Anton Dolin, Joyce Trisler and Paul Taylor. His theater designs have been seen at the Wimbledon Repertory in London, Provincetown Playhouse, North Shore Music Circus, Massachusetts, McCarter Theater in Princeton, Arena Stage in Buffalo and South Coast Rep in California. Mr. Tomlinson has designed over 100 television shows and 13 feature films. Since 1990 he has taught film and theater design at UCLA and the University of California at Irvine.

Ann Vachon graduated from The Juilliard School in 1961 and performed with the José Limón Dance Company from 1958 until 1975. She joined the Temple University dance faculty in 1978 where she coordinates the MFA program and teaches technique, repertory, dance composition and choreography. In 1981 she founded Dance Conduit, a Philadelphia-based dance company. She disbanded the company in 1993 in order to concentrate on special projects which have included her reconstruction of Limón's *Symphony for Strings*. In 1995 she earned a Master of Liberal Arts degree from Temple University and edited *Poland, 1946: the Photographs and Letters of John Vachon*, published by the Smithsonian Institution Press. She has taught and lectured on Limón in Mexico, Poland, Czechoslovakia and Taiwan, and is currently working with her son, Malachi Roth, on a feature-length documentary on Limón.

Charles Humphrey Woodford, son of Doris Humphrey, is the only living person to have experienced the daily life of the Humphrey-Weidman and Limón households. He is co-author of *Dance is a Moment: A Portrait of José Limón in Words and Pictures*, author of an essay on Doris Humphrey in *The International Encyclopedia of Modern Dance*, and co-editor of *The Vision of Modern Dance: In the Works of its Creators*. He is President of the Doris Humphrey Society and of Princeton Book Company, Publishers. He lives in New Jersey with his wife and four cats not far from the Limón barn and keeps in close touch with his grown children.

INDEX

A Choreographic Offering, 24, 33, 54, 55, 116, 117, 118, 120
Aitken, Hugh, 15
American Dance Festival (ADF), 2, 28, 33, 37, 38, 41, 55, 56, 85, 93, 113, 114
American Dance Theater, 5
ANTA, 94, 97, 101
Antigona, 79, 81
Ausdruckstanz, 67, 68

Bach, J.S., 9, 10, 11, 12, 13, 21, 37, 45, 91, 116
Balanchine, George, 4
Ballets Jooss, 61
Ballet Russe de Monte Carlo, 12
Barber, Samuel, 91
Barren Sceptre, 21
Bausch, Pina, 60
Beethoven, Ludwig van, 12
Bennington College, 46, 48
Berlioz, Hector, 12
Bettis, Valerie, 64
Bird, Dorothy, 64
Blue Roses, 93
Brahms, Johannes, 12
Brooks-Van Horn, 31

Capezio Dance Award, 104
Carlota, 2, 24, 81, 82, 121, 132
Cassandra, 105
Castro, Valentina, 78, 81
Cavell, Edith, 21
CENIDI Danza José Limón, 83
Central Intelligence Agency (CIA), 101, 102
Chaconne, 49, 71, 76, 91, 114, 117, 119
Charisse, Nanette, 64
Chavéz, Carlos, 79

Chopin, Frederic, 37, 87, 88, 89, 91, 123
Cohen, Selma Jeanne, 61
Concert, 87, 91
Condodina, Alice, 117
Connecticut College, 49, 55, 56, 60, 68, 85, 113, 116, 130
Copland, Aaron, 13, 16
Covarrubias, Miguel, 78, 79, 80, 81, 82
Culiacan, Mexico, 72, 83
Cunningham, Merce, 82, 93
Currier, Ruth, 4, 5, 23, 24, 88, 91, 114, 119, 123, 124

Dances, 85, 86, 89, 93
Dances at a Gathering, 93
Dances for Isadora, 24
Dance Players Studio, 37
Danzas Mexicanas, 76
Day on Earth, 16, 50, 105, 106
Dello Joio, Norman, 15
de Mille, Agnes, 13, 64
Denishawn Company, 27, 30
Dialogues, 79, 81, 92
Don Juan Fantasia, 91, 93
Duncan, Isadora, 11, 12, 18, 20, 24, 71

Empire State Festival, 15

Falco, Louis, 5, 15, 33, 119, 120
Fitz-Simmons, Foster, 27

Georgi, Yvonne, 61, 62
Graham, Martha, 4, 10, 12, 20, 37, 62, 64
Graham technique, 83
Group Theatre, 61

Hamilton, Peter, 30
Harkarvy, Benjamin, 121

Hatfield, Nellie, 28, 31
Hein, Marga, 45, 47, 48, 51
Hill, Martha, 18, 29, 37, 51, 120,
    127, 128
Hindemith, Paul, 16
Hollander, Michael, 123
House Committee on Un-American
    Activities (HUAC), 98, 107
Hoving, Lucas, 5, 16, 24, 33, 34, 59–70,
    71, 77, 91, 92, 105, 114, 122, 124, 125
Humphrey, Doris, 3, 5, 6, 7, 10, 11, 12,
    16, 20, 21, 30, 34, 38, 41, 45, 49, 51,
    60, 61, 62, 64, 65, 66, 67, 71, 75, 76,
    77, 81, 82, 91, 103, 105, 106, 107, 116,
    117, 118, 120
Humphrey-Weidman (Co.), 24, 30, 45,
    48, 51
Humphrey-Weidman School (Studio),
    30, 47, 64, 66, 71

Ide, Letitia, 91, 119
I, Odysseus, 114
Inquest, 20

Jacob's Pillow, 37, 47
Joiner, Betty, 48
Jones, Betty, 24, 65, 68, 71, 78, 81, 88,
    91, 93, 94, 114, 120, 123, 125
Jones, Bill T., 62
Jooss, Kurt, 61, 64, 65
José Limón Company, José Limón
    Dance Company, Limón Company,
    27, 30, 37, 41, 53, 54, 64, 83, 93, 114, 121
Jowitt, Deborah, 25
Juarez, Benito, 83
Juilliard School, Juilliard School of
    Music, 2, 16, 24, 29, 37, 41, 114, 120,
    121, 127, 128, 132
Juilliard Dance Theatre, 86

Kenetic Molpai, 66
Kisselgoff, Anna, 117, 125
Kodaly, Zoltan, 16, 18, 128
Koner, Pauline, 5, 24, 33, 68, 69, 71, 77,
    91, 92, 105, 114, 119, 122, 124, 125
Kreutzberg, Harald, 20, 61, 62, 68
Kuiper, Neel, 61

Laban, Rudolf von, 37, 61, 62
La Malinche, 33, 68, 77, 78, 82, 91, 103,
    105, 108
Lament for Ignacio Sanchez Mejias, 16,
    77, 91, 103
Leeder, Sigurd, 61
Legend, 24
Lewis, Daniel, 4, 71, 83
Library of Congress, 102
Lilac Garden, 13
Limón, Florencio, 60, 74
Limón Foundation, José Limón
    Dance Foundation, Limón Dance
    Foundation, 3, 94
Limón, Pauline, Pauline Lawrence,
    Pauline Lawrence Limón, 2, 28–35,
    45, 47, 48, 49, 50, 51, 66, 67, 92, 129,
    130, 131, 132
Limón, Traslaviña, 60, 72
Littlefield, Catherine, 64
Lloyd, Norman, 16
Los Quatros Soles, 78
Ludin, Fritz, 41, 43
Luxemburg, Rosa, 62

Magnussen, Jon, 121
Manchester, P.W., 92
Martin, John, 23, 77, 81, 103, 105, 106,
    107, 108
Massine, Leonide, 12
Maxwell, Carla, 83, 121, 123
May, Jim, 83
Mazurkas, 85–94, 123
McCallum, Harlan, 87, 123
McCarthy, Joseph, "McCarthyism",
    21, 98, 102
McDonagh, Don, 24
Michelangelo, 20, 37
Mills College, 48, 76
Ming Cho Lee, 33, 128
Missa Brevis, 16, 18, 23, 34, 54, 55, 86,
    113, 114, 120
Morgan, Barbara, 77
Muller, Jennifer, 120
Museum of Modern Art, MOMA, 102
Musical Offering, 120
My Son, My Enemy, 33

National Endowment for the Arts, NEA, 4, 109

National Institute of Fine Arts, 78

New Dance, Variations and Conclusion from New Dance, 11, 13, 105, 106, 108

New Dance Group, 61

New York State Council for the Arts, 54

Nielsen, Lavina, 64, 66, 92, 105

Night Spell, 34, 91, 105, 106

Nijinsky, Vaslav, 10

Novak, Lionel, 76

Ode to the Dance, 105

Odets, Clifford, 62

Office of War Information, 102

Ohio Ballet, 57

O'Neill Eugene, 15, 21

Orfeo, 2

Owen, Norton, 94

Palacio de Belles Artes, Belles Artes, 71, 82

Paul Taylor Company, 57

Passacaglia and Fugue in C Minor, 11, 12, 33, 81

Pavlova, Anna, 12

Payton, James, 94

Performing Arts International Exchange Program, International Exchange Program, 97, 101, 102

Pillar of Fire, 13

Pimsler, Susan, 30

Poll, Heinz, 57

Psalm, 23

Redes, 81

Reigger, Wallingford, 11, 13

Reinhardt, Max, 61

Reinhart, Charles and Stephanie, 41

Reyna, Rosa, 82

Ringside, 66

Rio Economic Conference, 99, 100, 108

Ritmo Jondo, 33, 103, 105, 106, 108

Robbins, Jerome, 93

Robert Joffrey Company, 57

Rodrigo, Florrie, 60, 61, 64

Rosenberg, Julius and Ethel, 69, 97, 98, 107

Ruins and Visions, 66, 105, 106, 108

Sadoff, Simon, 16, 30

Satyros, 105

Scherzo, 91

Schoenberg, Arnold, 13, 15, 91

Schuller, Gunther, 15, 91

Schulman, Alvin, 104, 105, 107, 108

Schuman, William, 128

Seckler, Beatrice, 64

Shakespeare, William, 21, 67

Shawn, Ted, 20, 66

Siegel, Marcia, 62

Sinaloa, Mexico, 59, 72

Skelton, Thomas, 28, 29, 53–58

Sokolow, Anna, 62, 82

Sorrell, Walter, 21

Stackhouse, Sarah, Sally Stackhouse, 15, 93, 94

State Academy of Music, Academia de Musica, 60, 72

St. Denis, Ruth, 20, 24

Stepanska, Cherny, 87

Stern, Isaac, 102

Story of Mankind, 105, 106, 108

Sweigard, Dr. Lulu, 37, 40, 41

Tamiris, Helen, 62

Tchaikovsky, Peter Ilyich, 11, 12

Tenebrae 1914, 23

Terry, Walter, 92, 107, 114

Theater Piece, 11

The Demon, 16

The Emporer Jones, 15, 21, 22, 55, 91, 114

The Exiles, 15, 91, 103, 105, 119, 120, 124

The Moor's Pavane, 4, 21, 29, 34, 55, 67, 68, 69, 83, 89, 91, 105, 106, 108, 117, 122, 124

The Traitor, 21, 34, 55, 68, 69, 70, 91, 103, 107, 113, 114, 120

The Unsung, 25, 82, 116, 121

The Visitation, 91, 103, 105, 106, 108, 113, 124

The War Between Men and Women, 49
The Winged, 24, 33, 120, 121
There is a Time, 22, 35, 41, 43, 51, 55, 66, 114, 118, 119
This Passion, 48
Tiger Rag, 27
Tonantzintla, 79, 81, 92
Touching the Souls, 68
Trisler, Joyce, 51

UNESCO, 97, 101, 103, 105
United States State Department, 71, 97, 98, 99, 100, 101, 102, 104, 108, 114, 120
US Cultural Exchange Program, 85
US Information Agency (USIA), 104, 107, 114, 120

Vachon, Ann, 93, 94
Venable, Lucy, 88, 94

Venza, Jac, 18
Villa-Lobos, Heitor, 15, 91
Vivaldi Concerto Grosso, Concerto Grosso, 105, 108, 117

Weidman, Charles, 3, 20, 30, 38, 45, 46, 47, 48, 49, 51, 64, 66, 75
Weidman Company, 49
White House, 34
Wigman, Mary, 61, 62, 68
Williams, Betty, 31
Wimmer, Lynn, 83
With My Red Fires, 11
Wolenski, Chester, 85, 88, 94, 123
Woodford, Charles F., 45
Woodford, Charles Humphrey, 13, 60
Wynne, David, 27

Zane, Arnie, 62
Zapata, Emilio, 60